MEXICAN COOKBOOK

for beginners

The Ultimate Collection of Authentic Mexican Recipes for Every Occasion – Easy, Quick, and Delicious Dishes for Tacos, Enchiladas, Burritos, Salsas, Quesadillas, Soups, Desserts, and More

Sophia del Sol

2025

Mexican Cookbook for Beginners: The Ultimate Collection of Authentic Mexican Recipes in English for Every Occasion – Easy, Quick, and Delicious Dishes for Tacos, Enchiladas, Burritos, Salsas, Quesadillas, Soups, Desserts, and More

Copyright © 2025 Sophia del Sol
All rights reserved.

No part of this publication may be reproduced, distributed, or transmitted in any form or by any means, including photocopying, recording, or other electronic or mechanical methods, without the prior written permission of the publisher, except in the case of brief quotations used in reviews or articles.

Disclaimer

This book is for informational purposes only. Th e author and publisher make no representations or warranties regarding the accuracy or completeness of the content. While every effort has been made to ensure the recipes and instructions are accurate, results may vary based on individual cooking techniques, kitchen equipment, and ingredient availability. Readers should exercise their own discretion and follow appropriate safety measures when preparing food.

Trademarks

All product names, brand names, and trademarks mentioned in this book are the property of their respective owners. Their inclusion does not imply affiliation with or endorsement by the author or publisher.

First Edition

Table of Contents

STAPLES & BASICS

Fresh Pico de Gallo	6
Guacamole	7
Roasted Tomatillo Salsa (Salsa Verde)	8
Basic Red Salsa	9
Cilantro Lime Crema	10
Chipotle Mayo	11
Mexican Crema Substitute	12
Quick Red Enchilada Sauce	13
Easy Mole Sauce	14
Pickled Red Onions	15
Salsa Roja Taquera (Taco-Style Red Salsa)	16
Jalapeño Hot Sauce	17
Refried Beans	18
Simple Mexican Rice	19
Corn Tortillas (Homemade Shortcut Recipe)	20

BREAKFAST FAVORITES

Huevos Rancheros	21
Mexican Scrambled Eggs (Huevos a la Mexicana)	22
Chilaquiles Verdes (with Store-Bought Tortilla Chips)	23
Breakfast Burritos	24
Breakfast Quesadillas	25
Mexican Fruit Salad with Tajín	26
Mexican Coffee (Café de Olla)	27
Avocado Toast with Lime and Cilantro	28
Sweet Corn Tamales (Tamales de Elote)	29
Soups & Comfort Bowls	30

EASY TORTILLA SOUP

Black Bean Soup with Lime	31
Mexican Chicken Soup (Caldo de Pollo)	32
Pozole Rojo (Simplified Version)	33
Albondigas Soup (Mexican Meatball Soup)	34
Mexican Rice Soup	35
Frijoles de la Olla (Simple Stewed Beans)	36
Chicken and Hominy Soup (Caldo de Maíz)	37
Sopa de Fideo (Mexican Vermicelli Soup)	38

STREET FOOD & SNACKS

Ground Beef Tacos	39
Chicken Tinga Tacos	40
Baja Fish Tacos	41
Shrimp Tacos with Garlic Lime Sauce	42
Elote (Mexican Street Corn)	43
Nachos with Pico de Gallo and Cheese Sauce	44
Queso Fundido with Chorizo	45
Gorditas with Refried Beans	46
Sopes with Chicken or Veggies	47
Chicken Flautas (Crispy Rolled Tacos)	48
Mexican Street Tostadas	49

MAIN DISHES (PLATOS FUERTES) MEAT & POULTRY

Carne Asada (Grilled Beef)	50
Chicken Fajitas	51
Sheet Pan Chicken Enchiladas	52
Slow Cooker Carnitas (Pulled Pork)	53
Ground Turkey Tacos	54
Beef Enchiladas with Red Sauce	55
Pollo Asado (Grilled Marinated Chicken)	56

MAIN DISHES (PLATOS FUERTES) SEAFOOD

Shrimp Fajitas	57
Baja Fish Burritos	58
Simple Ceviche (Shrimp or White Fish)	59
Garlic Butter Shrimp Tacos	60
Veracruz-Style Fish (Pescado a la Veracruzana)	61

MAIN DISHES (PLATOS FUERTES) VEGETARIAN

Vegetarian Enchiladas with Black Beans	62
Sweet Potato Tacos with Chipotle Crema	63
Veggie Quesadillas	64
Mexican Zucchini Boats	65
Stuffed Bell Peppers with Mexican Rice and Beans	66

DESSERTS & DRINKS

Mexican Hot Chocolate	67
Tres Leches Cake	68
Churros with Chocolate Sauce	69
Rice Pudding (Arroz con Leche)	70
Horchata (Sweet Rice Milk Drink)	71
Flan (Mexican Caramel Custard)	72
Pineapple Tamales (Tamales de Piña)	73
Fried Ice Cream with Cinnamon Sugar	74
Margarita Mocktail (Non-Alcoholic Option)	75

Some recipes include simplified options like sour cream or mayonnaise-based sauces to help beginners build confidence. Authentic alternatives are also suggested throughout the book whenever possible.

Fresh Pico de Gallo

Servings: 4 | Prep Time: 10 minutes | Cook Time: 0 minutes

Ingredients:

- 2 medium tomatoes, finely chopped
- 1/2 medium red onion, finely chopped
- 1/4 cup (60 ml) fresh cilantro, chopped
- 1 small jalapeño, deseeded and finely chopped
- 1 tbsp (15 ml) fresh lime juice
- 1/4 tsp salt
- [Optional] 1 clove garlic, minced

Instructions:

1. **Chop** the tomatoes, red onion, cilantro, and jalapeño into small, uniform pieces.
2. **Place** all chopped ingredients in a medium bowl.
3. **Add** lime juice and salt. If using, add the minced garlic for extra flavor.
4. **Stir** gently until everything is well mixed.
5. **Taste** and adjust seasoning with more salt or lime if needed.
6. **Serve** immediately or refrigerate for up to 2 hours before serving for the flavors to meld.

Guacamole

~150 kcal per serving

Servings: 4 | Prep Time: 10 minutes | Cook Time: 0 minutes

Ingredients:

- 3 ripe avocados, peeled and pitted
- 1/2 small red onion, finely chopped
- 1 medium tomato, deseeded and chopped
- 1/4 cup (60 ml) fresh cilantro, chopped
- 1 small jalapeño, deseeded and finely chopped
- 1 tbsp (15 ml) fresh lime juice
- 1/4 tsp salt
- [Optional] 1 clove garlic, minced

Instructions:

1. **Mash** the avocados in a medium bowl using a fork or potato masher until smooth but slightly chunky.
2. **Add** the red onion, tomato, cilantro, jalapeño, lime juice, and salt.
3. **Mix** everything together until well combined.
4. **Taste** and adjust seasoning with more lime or salt if needed.
5. **Serve** immediately with tortilla chips or as a topping for tacos, burritos, or grilled meats.

Roasted Tomatillo Salsa (Salsa Verde)

Servings: 4 | Prep Time: 10 minutes | Cook Time: 15 minutes

~25 kcal per serving

Ingredients:

- 6 medium tomatillos, husked and rinsed
- 1 small onion, quartered
- 2 cloves garlic, unpeeled
- 1-2 small jalapeños, stems removed
- 1/4 cup (60 ml) fresh cilantro, chopped
- 1 tbsp (15 ml) fresh lime juice
- 1/4 tsp salt
- [Optional] 1/4 tsp ground cumin

Instructions:

1. **Preheat** your oven to 400°F (200°C).
2. **Place** the tomatillos, onion, garlic, and jalapeños on a baking sheet in a single layer.
3. **Roast** in the oven for 10-12 minutes, or until the tomatillos are soft and slightly charred.
4. **Remove** the garlic cloves from the skins and transfer all the roasted ingredients to a blender or food processor.
5. **Add** the cilantro, lime juice, salt, and optional cumin to the blender.
6. **Blend** until smooth, adding a little water if needed to reach your desired consistency.
7. **Taste** and adjust seasoning with more salt or lime if necessary.
8. **Serve** immediately with tortilla chips or as a topping for tacos, grilled meats, or burritos.

Basic Red Salsa

Servings: 4 | Prep Time: 10 minutes | Cook Time: 0 minutes

Ingredients:

- 4 medium ripe tomatoes, chopped
- 1/4 small red onion, finely chopped
- 1 small jalapeño, deseeded and finely chopped
- 1/4 cup (60 ml) fresh cilantro, chopped
- 1 tbsp (15 ml) fresh lime juice
- 1/4 tsp salt
- [Optional] 1/2 tsp ground cumin

Instructions:

1. **Chop** the tomatoes, onion, and jalapeño into small, uniform pieces.
2. **Place** all chopped ingredients into a medium bowl.
3. **Add** the cilantro, lime juice, salt, and optional cumin.
4. **Mix** everything together until well combined.
5. **Taste** and adjust seasoning with more salt or lime if needed.
6. **Serve** immediately with tortilla chips, tacos, or any dish that needs a fresh, flavorful kick.

Cilantro Lime Crema

per serving

Servings: 4 | Prep Time: 5 minutes | Cook Time: 0 minutes

Ingredients:

- 1/2 cup (120 ml) sour cream
- 1/4 cup (60 ml) mayonnaise
- 2 tbsp (30 ml) fresh lime juice
- 1/4 cup (60 ml) fresh cilantro, chopped
- 1/4 tsp salt
- [Optional] 1/4 tsp garlic powder

Instructions:

1. **Combine** the sour cream and mayonnaise in a small bowl.
2. **Add** the lime juice, cilantro, salt, and optional garlic powder.
3. **Mix** everything together until smooth and well combined.
4. **Taste** and adjust seasoning with more lime juice or salt if needed.
5. **Serve** immediately or refrigerate for up to 2 hours to allow the flavors to meld.

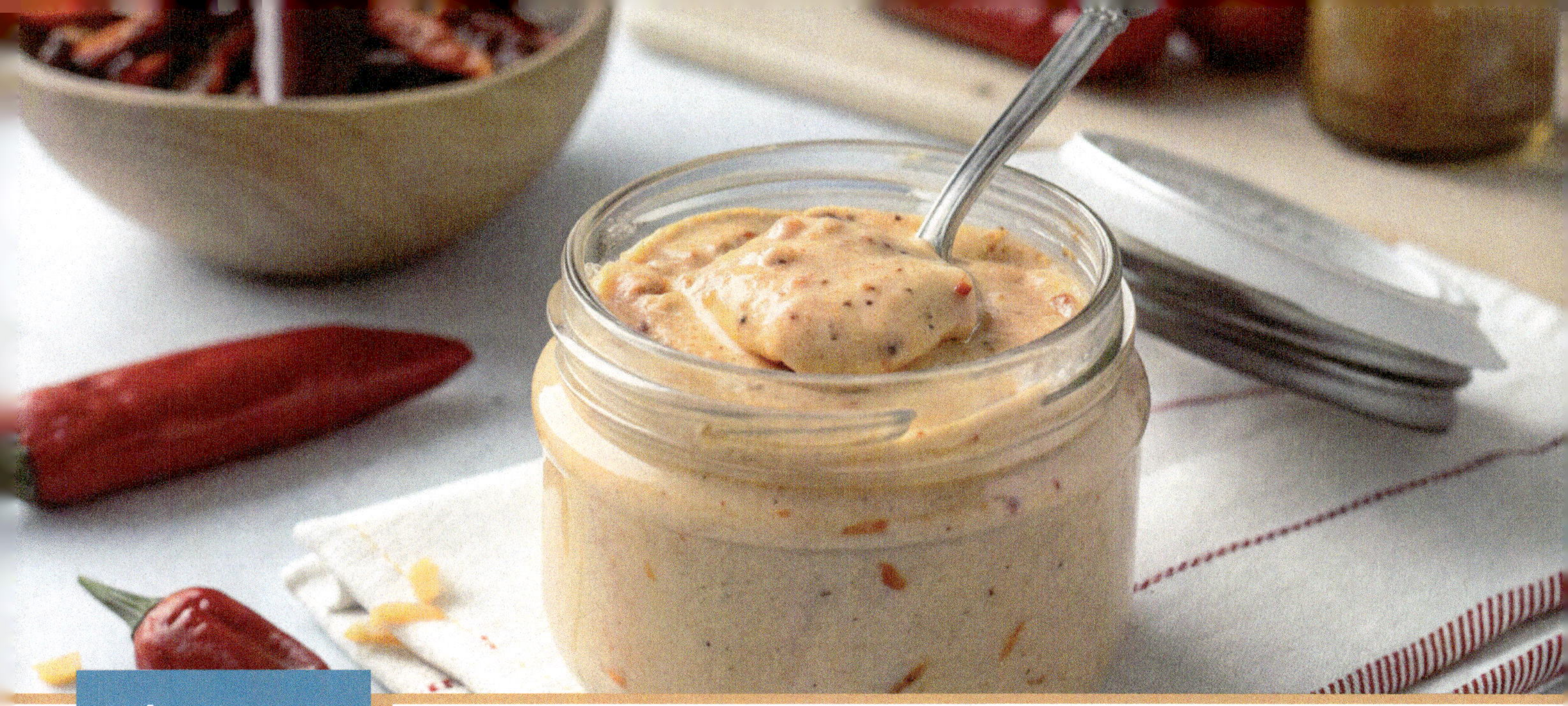

Chipotle Mayo

~90 kcal per serving

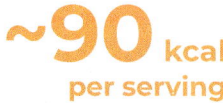

Servings: 4 | Prep Time: 5 minutes | Cook Time: 0 minutes

Ingredients:

- 1/2 cup (120 ml) mayonnaise
- 1 tbsp (15 ml) fresh lime juice
- 1-2 tbsp (15-30 ml) chipotle peppers in adobo sauce, chopped
- 1/4 tsp garlic powder
- 1/4 tsp salt

Instructions:

1. **Combine** the mayonnaise and lime juice in a small bowl.
2. **Add** the chopped chipotle peppers, garlic powder, and salt.
3. **Mix** everything together until smooth and well blended.
4. **Taste** and adjust the spice level by adding more chipotle peppers or lime juice if needed.
5. **Serve** immediately or refrigerate for up to 2 hours to let the flavors develop.

Mexican Crema Substitute

Servings: 4 | Prep Time: 5 minutes | Cook Time: 0 minutes

Ingredients:

- 1/2 cup (120 ml) sour cream
- 1/4 cup (60 ml) heavy cream
- 1 tbsp (15 ml) fresh lime juice
- 1/4 tsp salt

Instructions:

1. **Combine** the sour cream and heavy cream in a small bowl.
2. **Add** the lime juice and salt.
3. **Mix** until smooth and well combined.
4. **Taste** and adjust seasoning with more lime juice or salt if needed.
5. **Serve** immediately or refrigerate for up to 2 days.

Quick Red Enchilada Sauce

Servings: 4 | Prep Time: 5 minutes | Cook Time: 10 minutes

Ingredients:

- 2 tbsp (30 ml) vegetable oil
- 1/4 cup (40 g) chili powder
- 1/2 tsp garlic powder
- 1/2 tsp onion powder
- 1/4 tsp ground cumin
- 1/4 tsp salt
- 1 (8 oz / 225 g) can tomato sauce
- 1 cup (240 ml) water
- 1 tbsp (15 ml) fresh lime juice

Instructions:

1. **Heat** the vegetable oil in a medium saucepan over medium heat.
2. **Add** the chili powder, garlic powder, onion powder, cumin, and salt.
3. **Stir** the spices into the oil and cook for 1-2 minutes to bring out their flavors.
4. **Pour** in the tomato sauce and water, stirring to combine.
5. **Bring** the mixture to a simmer and cook for 5-7 minutes, stirring occasionally, until thickened.
6. **Add** the lime juice and stir to combine.
7. **Taste** and adjust seasoning with more salt or lime juice if needed.
8. **Serve** immediately over enchiladas, tacos, or your favorite Mexican dishes.

Easy Mole Sauce

Servings: 4 | Prep Time: 10 minutes | Cook Time: 15 minutes

Ingredients:

- 2 tbsp (30 ml) vegetable oil
- 1/4 cup (40 g) chili powder
- 1/4 cup (40 g) unsweetened cocoa powder
- 1 tbsp (15 g) sesame seeds
- 1/4 tsp ground cumin
- 1/4 tsp ground cinnamon
- 1/2 tsp garlic powder
- 1/2 tsp onion powder
- 1/4 tsp salt
- 1 cup (240 ml) chicken broth
- 1/4 cup (60 ml) tomato paste
- 1 tbsp (15 ml) brown sugar
- 1 tbsp (15 ml) fresh lime juice

Instructions:

1. **Heat** the vegetable oil in a medium saucepan over medium heat.
2. **Add** the chili powder, cocoa powder, sesame seeds, cumin, cinnamon, garlic powder, onion powder, and salt. Stir to combine and cook for 1-2 minutes to bring out the flavors.
3. **Pour** in the chicken broth and tomato paste, stirring until smooth.
4. **Add** the brown sugar and lime juice, mixing well.
5. **Bring** the sauce to a simmer, and cook for 10 minutes, stirring occasionally, until thickened.
6. **Taste** and adjust seasoning with more salt or sugar if needed.
7. **Serve** over chicken, enchiladas, tacos, or any dish that could use a rich, flavorful mole sauce.

Pickled Red Onions

Servings: 6 | Prep Time: 10 minutes | Cook Time: 5 minutes

Ingredients:

- 1 large (200 g) red onion, thinly sliced
- 1/2 cup (120 ml) white vinegar
- 1/2 cup (120 ml) water
- 1 tbsp (15 g) sugar
- 1 tsp (5 g) salt
- 1 garlic clove, smashed
- 1/2 tsp (1 g) whole black peppercorns
- 1/2 tsp (1 g) dried oregano
- 1/4 tsp (1 g) red pepper flakes (optional)

Instructions:

1. **Slice** the red onion thinly and set aside in a medium-sized jar or bowl.
2. **In a small saucepan,** combine the vinegar, water, sugar, salt, garlic, peppercorns, oregano, and red pepper flakes (if using).
3. **Bring** the mixture to a simmer over medium heat, stirring occasionally to dissolve the sugar and salt. Let it simmer for about 3-5 minutes.
4. **Pour** the hot vinegar mixture over the sliced onions. Stir to coat the onions evenly.
5. **Let** the onions sit for about 10 minutes at room temperature to pickle.
6. **Serve** the pickled red onions immediately or store in the refrigerator for up to 2 weeks.

Salsa Roja Taquera (Taco-Style Red Salsa)

~40 kcal per serving

Servings: 6 | Prep Time: 10 minutes | Cook Time: 5 minutes

Ingredients:

- 2 medium (250 g) Roma tomatoes, halved
- 1/2 medium (60 g) white onion, quartered
- 2 (10 g) dried guajillo chiles, stemmed and seeded
- 1 (2 g) dried pasilla chile, stemmed and seeded
- 1 garlic clove, peeled
- 1/2 tsp (2 g) salt, or to taste
- 1/4 tsp (1 g) ground cumin (optional)
- 1/2 cup (120 ml) water

Instructions:

1. **Toast** the dried guajillo and pasilla chiles in a dry skillet over medium heat for about 1-2 minutes, until fragrant. Be careful not to burn them.
2. **Remove** the chiles from the skillet and place them in a bowl. Cover with hot water and let them soak for about 5 minutes, or until softened.
3. **In the same skillet,** add the halved tomatoes, onion, and garlic. Roast them over medium heat for about 3-4 minutes, turning occasionally, until the tomatoes are charred and the onion is softened.
4. **Drain** the chiles and add them to a blender along with the roasted tomatoes, onion, garlic, salt, cumin (if using), and water.
5. **Blend** everything together until smooth. Taste and adjust salt if necessary.
6. **Serve** your Salsa Roja Taquera as a topping for tacos, grilled meats, or even roasted vegetables.

Jalapeño Hot Sauce

~15 kcal per serving

Servings: 6 | Prep Time: 5 minutes | Cook Time: 10 minutes

Ingredients:

- 6 fresh (150 g) jalapeño peppers, stemmed and roughly chopped
- 1/2 medium (60 g) white onion, chopped
- 2 garlic cloves, peeled
- 1/2 cup (120 ml) white vinegar
- 1/4 cup (60 ml) water
- 1/2 tsp (2 g) salt, or to taste
- 1/4 tsp (1 g) sugar (optional, for balancing heat)
- 1 tbsp (15 ml) olive oil

Instructions:

1. **Heat** the olive oil in a small saucepan over medium heat. Add the chopped onions and garlic, cooking for about 2 minutes until softened.
2. **Add** the chopped jalapeños to the pan and cook for another 3 minutes, allowing them to release their oils and become slightly tender.
3. **Pour** in the vinegar and water, then add the salt and sugar (if using). Stir everything together.
4. **Bring** the mixture to a simmer and cook for an additional 3-4 minutes. Remove from heat and let it cool slightly.
5. **Transfer** the mixture to a blender and blend until smooth. Taste and adjust the seasoning if needed.
6. **Serve** your Jalapeño Hot Sauce as a zesty topping for tacos, grilled meats, or roasted vegetables.

Refried Beans

Servings: 6 | Prep Time: 10 minutes | Cook Time: 30 minutes

~180 kcal per serving

Ingredients:

- 2 cups (450 g) dried pinto beans (or use 4 cups of canned beans)
- 1/2 medium (60 g) onion, chopped
- 2 garlic cloves, minced
- 2 tbsp (30 ml) vegetable oil or lard
- 1/2 tsp (2 g) ground cumin
- 1/4 tsp (1 g) ground black pepper
- Salt to taste
- 4 cups (960 ml) water (or as needed for cooking)

Instructions:

1. **Rinse** the dried pinto beans thoroughly under cold water. In a large pot, cover the beans with water, making sure there's about 2 inches of water above the beans.
2. **Bring** the beans to a boil over medium-high heat. Once boiling, reduce the heat to low and let them simmer for 1.5-2 hours, or until soft. (Skip this step if using canned beans.)
3. **Drain** the beans, reserving some of the cooking liquid for later use. Set the beans aside.
4. **Heat** the vegetable oil (or lard) in a large skillet over medium heat. Add the chopped onion and cook for 3-4 minutes until softened.
5. **Add** the minced garlic and cook for an additional minute until fragrant.
6. **Mash** the beans with a potato masher or the back of a spoon, adding a bit of the reserved cooking liquid (or water) as needed for desired consistency. You can leave them a bit chunky or mash them smooth.
7. **Add** the mashed beans to the skillet with the onion and garlic mixture. Stir in the cumin, black pepper, and salt to taste.
8. **Fry** the beans for about 10 minutes, stirring occasionally, until they reach a creamy and slightly thick consistency. Add more liquid if needed.
9. **Serve** your Refried Beans warm as a perfect side for tacos, burritos, or as a dip for chips.

Simple Mexican Rice

~210 kcal per serving

Servings: 4 | Prep Time: 5 minutes | Cook Time: 20 minutes

Ingredients:

- 1 cup (200 g) long-grain white rice
- 2 tbsp (30 ml) vegetable oil
- 1/4 cup (60 g) onion, finely chopped
- 1 garlic clove, minced
- 1 1/2 cups (360 ml) chicken or vegetable broth
- 1/2 cup (120 ml) tomato sauce
- 1/2 tsp (2 g) ground cumin
- 1/4 tsp (1 g) ground black pepper
- Salt to taste
- 1/4 cup (15 g) fresh cilantro, chopped (optional)

Instructions:

1. **Rinse** the rice under cold water until the water runs clear, then drain.
2. **Heat** the vegetable oil in a medium-sized pot over medium heat. Add the rice and cook for 2-3 minutes, stirring occasionally, until the rice is lightly toasted and golden.
3. **Add** the chopped onion and minced garlic to the pot. Cook for an additional 2 minutes, stirring frequently, until the onion becomes soft and translucent.
4. **Pour** in the chicken or vegetable broth, tomato sauce, ground cumin, black pepper, and salt to taste. Stir everything together.
5. **Bring** the mixture to a boil. Once boiling, reduce the heat to low, cover, and let the rice simmer for 15-18 minutes, or until all the liquid is absorbed and the rice is tender.
6. **Fluff** the rice with a fork to separate the grains. If desired, stir in the chopped fresh cilantro for added flavor and color.
7. **Serve** your Simple Mexican Rice as a delicious side dish for tacos, enchiladas, or grilled meats.

Corn Tortillas (Homemade Shortcut Recipe)

Servings: 10 | Prep Time: 5 minutes | Cook Time: 10 minutes

~**120** kcal per serving

Ingredients:

- 2 cups (240 g) masa harina (corn flour for tortillas)
- 1/2 tsp (2 g) salt
- 1 1/4 cups (300 ml) warm water (adjust as needed)
- 1 tbsp (15 ml) vegetable oil (optional for softer tortillas)

Instructions:

1. **Combine** the masa harina and salt in a large mixing bowl.
2. **Add** the warm water gradually, mixing with your hands until the dough starts to come together. If the dough is too dry, add a little more water, 1 tablespoon at a time. If too sticky, add a little more masa harina.
3. **Knead** the dough for 1-2 minutes until it's smooth and pliable. Cover it with a damp cloth and let it rest for 10 minutes.
4. **Divide** the dough into 10 equal portions and roll each into a ball.
5. **Preheat** a cast-iron skillet or griddle over medium-high heat.
6. **Flatten** each dough ball into a round tortilla using a tortilla press, rolling pin, or your hands. Aim for a thin, even thickness, about 6 inches in diameter.
7. **Cook** each tortilla on the hot skillet for about 1 minute on each side, or until brown spots appear and the tortilla puffs slightly.
8. **Remove** the cooked tortillas and place them in a clean kitchen towel to keep warm.
9. **Serve** your homemade corn tortillas with tacos, enchiladas, or as a side to any Mexican meal.

Breakfast Favorites

Huevos Rancheros

~350 kcal per serving

Servings: 2 | Prep Time: 10 minutes | Cook Time: 20 minutes

Ingredients:

- 2 tbsp (30 ml) vegetable oil
- 1 cup (160 g) diced onion
- 2 cloves garlic, minced
- 1/2 cup (120 ml) tomato sauce
- 1 cup (240 ml) canned crushed tomatoes
- 1 tsp chili powder
- 1/2 tsp ground cumin
- 1/4 tsp paprika
- Salt, to taste
- Freshly ground black pepper, to taste
- 1/4 cup (60 ml) water
- 4 large eggs
- 4 corn tortillas
- 1 cup (100 g) shredded Mexican cheese (like Oaxaca or Monterey Jack)
- Optional: Fresh cilantro, chopped, for garnish
- Optional: Sliced avocado, hot sauce, or sour cream for serving

Instructions:

1. **Heat the oil** in a large skillet over medium heat. Add the diced onion and cook, stirring occasionally, until it becomes translucent, about 5 minutes.
2. **Stir in the garlic** and cook for another minute, until fragrant.
3. **Add the tomato sauce, crushed tomatoes, chili powder, cumin, paprika, salt, and black pepper** to the skillet. Mix everything together well.
4. **Reduce the heat** and simmer the sauce for about 10 minutes, stirring occasionally, until it thickens slightly. Add the water and stir until combined.
5. **Warm the tortillas** on a separate skillet over medium heat, about 1 minute on each side. Keep warm.
6. **Fry the eggs** : In another skillet, heat a bit of vegetable oil over medium heat. Crack the eggs into the skillet and cook until the whites are set but the yolks are still runny, about 2-3 minutes.
7. **Divide the tortillas** between two plates. Spoon some of the tomato sauce over each tortilla, spreading evenly.
8. **Place a fried egg** on top of each tortilla. Sprinkle with shredded cheese.
9. **Cover the skillet** with a lid and cook for an additional minute or until the cheese is melted.
10. **Serve** with fresh cilantro, avocado slices, hot sauce, and/or a dollop of sour cream if desired.

Mexican Scrambled Eggs (Huevos a la Mexicana)

~250 kcal per serving

Servings: 2 | Prep Time: 10 minutes | Cook Time: 5 minutes

Ingredients:

- 4 large eggs
- 1 tbsp (15 ml) vegetable oil
- 1/2 cup (75 g) diced tomato
- 1/4 cup (40 g) diced onion
- 1/4 cup (30 g) diced bell pepper (optional)
- 1-2 serrano or jalapeño peppers, finely chopped
- Salt, to taste
- Freshly ground black pepper, to taste
- 1/4 cup (30 g) crumbled queso fresco or shredded cheddar (optional)
- Fresh cilantro, chopped, for garnish

Instructions:

1. **Crack the eggs** into a bowl and whisk them together with a pinch of salt and black pepper. Set aside.
2. **Heat the oil** in a skillet over medium heat. Add the diced onion and bell pepper (if using). Sauté for 2-3 minutes, until the vegetables soften.
3. **Add the diced tomato and chopped serrano or jalapeño peppers** to the skillet. Cook for an additional 2 minutes, stirring occasionally, until the tomatoes begin to soften and release their juices.
4. **Pour the beaten eggs** into the skillet with the vegetables. Let them sit for a few seconds, then gently stir and scramble the eggs. Continue cooking for another 2-3 minutes, stirring occasionally, until the eggs are fully cooked and soft but not dry.
5. **Remove from heat** and stir in the crumbled queso fresco or shredded cheddar (if using).
6. **Garnish with fresh cilantro** and serve immediately with warm tortillas or as a side with your favorite breakfast.

Chilaquiles Verdes (with Store-Bought Tortilla Chips)

~450 kcal per serving

Servings: 2 | Prep Time: 10 minutes | Cook Time: 10 minutes

Ingredients:

- 2 cups (150 g) store-bought tortilla chips
- 1 cup (240 ml) green salsa (salsa verde)
- 1/4 cup (60 ml) water or chicken broth
- 1 tbsp (15 ml) vegetable oil
- 1/2 cup (75 g) diced onion
- 1/4 cup (30 g) chopped fresh cilantro
- 2 large eggs
- 1/4 cup (30 g) crumbled queso fresco
- Sour cream, for garnish (optional)
- 1 lime, cut into wedges
- [Optional] 1/2 cup (60 g) shredded chicken or beef

Instructions:

1. **Heat the oil** in a large skillet over medium heat. Add the diced onion and sauté for 2-3 minutes until softened and translucent.
2. **Add the green salsa** to the skillet, along with the water or chicken broth. Stir and bring to a simmer. Let it cook for 2-3 minutes, until the sauce is heated through.
3. **Stir in the tortilla chips**, making sure they are well-coated with the salsa. Let the chips soak in the sauce for 1-2 minutes, so they soften slightly but still retain some crunch.
4. **In a separate pan, fry the eggs** to your preference (sunny side up, scrambled, or over-easy).
5. **Add the shredded chicken or beef** (if using) to the skillet with the chips and salsa, and cook for an additional 1-2 minutes until heated through.
6. **Serve the chilaquiles** by placing a portion on each plate. Top with a fried egg, crumbled queso fresco, fresh cilantro, and a dollop of sour cream.
7. **Garnish with lime wedges** on the side, and enjoy your quick and delicious Chilaquiles Verdes!

Breakfast Burritos

Servings: 2 | Prep Time: 10 minutes | Cook Time: 10 minutes

Ingredients:

- 4 large eggs
- 1/2 cup (60 g) shredded cheddar cheese
- 1/4 cup (60 g) diced onion
- 1/4 cup (60 g) diced bell pepper
- 2 tbsp (30 ml) vegetable oil
- 1/2 cup (75 g) cooked breakfast sausage, crumbled
- 1/4 cup (60 g) salsa
- 2 large flour tortillas
- 1/4 cup (30 g) sour cream
- [Optional] 1/4 cup (30 g) sliced avocado
- [Optional] 1/4 tsp ground cumin or chili powder

Instructions:

1. **Heat the oil** in a large skillet over medium heat. Add the diced onion and bell pepper, and sauté for 3-4 minutes until softened.
2. **Add the crumbled sausage** to the skillet and cook for an additional 2-3 minutes until browned. If you're using optional spices like cumin or chili powder, add them now.
3. **Whisk the eggs** in a bowl, then pour them into the skillet with the vegetables and sausage. Scramble the eggs until fully cooked, about 3-4 minutes.
4. **Warm the tortillas** by placing them in a dry skillet or microwave for a few seconds until soft and pliable.
5. **Assemble the burritos**: Place the egg mixture in the center of each tortilla, then top with shredded cheddar cheese and salsa.
6. **Roll the tortillas** by folding in the sides and rolling them up tightly to enclose the filling.
7. **Serve** your breakfast burritos with a side of sour cream and optional avocado slices. Enjoy a hearty, flavorful breakfast on the go!

Breakfast Quesadillas

Servings: 2 | Prep Time: 10 minutes | Cook Time: 10 minutes

Ingredients:

- 2 large flour tortillas
- 1/2 cup (60 g) shredded cheddar cheese
- 1/2 cup (60 g) scrambled eggs (about 2 eggs)
- 1/4 cup (30 g) cooked breakfast sausage, crumbled
- 1/4 cup (30 g) diced bell peppers
- 1/4 cup (30 g) diced onion
- 2 tbsp (30 ml) vegetable oil
- 1/4 cup (60 g) salsa
- [Optional] 1/4 tsp ground cumin or chili powder
- [Optional] 1/4 cup (30 g) sour cream for dipping

Instructions:

1. **Prepare the scrambled eggs** : Whisk 2 eggs in a bowl and cook them in a skillet over medium heat, stirring frequently, until fully scrambled. Set aside.
2. **Cook the vegetables** : In the same skillet, heat 1 tablespoon of oil and sauté the diced bell peppers and onions until soft, about 3 minutes. Set aside.
3. **Assemble the quesadillas** : Lay a tortilla flat and sprinkle half of the shredded cheddar cheese over the surface. Top with half of the scrambled eggs, cooked sausage, and sautéed bell peppers and onions. Sprinkle a pinch of cumin or chili powder if desired.
4. **Grill the quesadilla** : Heat 1 tablespoon of oil in the skillet over medium heat. Place the assembled quesadilla in the skillet and cook for 2-3 minutes, pressing gently, until the bottom is golden and crispy. Flip and cook the other side for another 2-3 minutes until golden and the cheese is melted.
5. **Serve** : Cut the quesadilla into wedges and serve with salsa and sour cream for dipping.

Mexican Fruit Salad with Tajín

Servings: 4 | Prep Time: 10 minutes | Cook Time: 0 minutes

Ingredients:

- 1 cup (150 g) diced watermelon
- 1 cup (150 g) diced pineapple
- 1 cup (150 g) diced mango
- 1/2 cup (75 g) diced cucumber
- 1/2 cup (75 g) orange segments
- 1 tbsp (15 ml) fresh lime juice
- 1 tsp (2 g) Tajín seasoning
- [Optional] 1 tbsp (15 ml) honey or agave syrup

Instructions:

1. **Prepare the fruit** : Dice the watermelon, pineapple, mango, cucumber, and orange into bite-sized pieces.
2. **Combine the ingredients** : In a large mixing bowl, combine all the diced fruits and cucumber.
3. **Add the flavor** : Drizzle with fresh lime juice and sprinkle with Tajín seasoning. Stir gently to coat the fruit evenly.
4. **Optional sweetness** : For a touch of sweetness, drizzle honey or agave syrup over the salad and mix again.
5. **Serve** : Serve immediately as a refreshing breakfast or light snack.

Mexican Coffee (Café de Olla)

~120 kcal per serving

Servings: 4 | Prep Time: 5 minutes | Cook Time: 15 minutes

Ingredients:

- 4 cups (960 ml) water
- 1/2 cup (50 g) ground Mexican coffee (preferably café de olla style or a dark roast)
- 2-3 cinnamon sticks
- 1/4 cup (60 g) piloncillo or dark brown sugar (grated)
- [Optional] 1-2 cloves
- [Optional] 1 tsp (5 ml) vanilla extract

Instructions:

1. **Prepare the base** : In a medium pot, bring the water to a boil over medium heat.
2. **Add the spices** : Add the cinnamon sticks (and cloves, if using) to the boiling water, and simmer for 5 minutes to release their aroma and flavor.
3. **Brew the coffee** : Add the ground coffee to the pot and stir to combine with the cinnamon. Let it simmer for an additional 5 minutes, ensuring the coffee brews properly.
4. **Sweeten the coffee** : Add the grated piloncillo or brown sugar to the pot, and stir until fully dissolved. You can adjust the sweetness to your liking.
5. **Strain and serve** : Remove the cinnamon sticks and strain the coffee into mugs. If desired, add vanilla extract for extra flavor.
6. **Enjoy** : Serve hot and enjoy this warm, flavorful Mexican coffee with your breakfast!

Avocado Toast with Lime and Cilantro

Servings: 2 | Prep Time: 5 minutes | Cook Time: 5 minutes

Ingredients:

- 2 slices of whole grain or sourdough bread
- 1 ripe avocado
- 1 lime (juice only)
- 1 tbsp (15 g) fresh cilantro, chopped
- 1/4 tsp salt
- [Optional] 1/4 tsp ground black pepper
- [Optional] 1-2 slices of jalapeño for a spicy kick

Instructions:

1. **Toast the bread** : Toast the slices of bread until golden and crisp. You can use a toaster, a grill pan, or a skillet.
2. **Prepare the avocado** : While the bread is toasting, cut the avocado in half, remove the pit, and scoop the flesh into a bowl.
3. **Mash the avocado** : Mash the avocado with a fork until smooth, leaving it a bit chunky if you prefer.
4. **Flavor the avocado** : Add the lime juice, chopped cilantro, salt, and pepper (if using) to the mashed avocado. Stir to combine.
5. **Assemble the toast** : Spread the avocado mixture evenly on the toasted bread slices.
6. **Garnish and serve** : If desired, top with slices of jalapeño for extra flavor and heat.
7. **Enjoy** : Serve immediately for a delicious, fresh, and satisfying breakfast!

Sweet Corn Tamales (Tamales de Elote)

Servings: 12 tamales | Prep Time: 20 minutes | Cook Time: 1 hour 30 minutes

Ingredients:

- 2 cups (300 g) masa harina for tamales
- 1 cup (240 ml) whole milk
- 1/2 cup (120 g) unsalted butter, softened
- 1/2 cup (100 g) sugar
- 1 1/2 cups (180 g) fresh corn kernels (or frozen corn, thawed)
- 1 tsp (5 g) vanilla extract
- 1/2 tsp (2 g) baking powder
- 1/4 tsp (1 g) salt
- 12 corn husks, soaked in warm water for 30 minutes
- [Optional] 1/4 tsp cinnamon for extra flavor

Instructions:

1. **Prepare the corn husks** : Soak the corn husks in warm water for 30 minutes to make them pliable. Drain and set aside.
2. **Mix the masa dough** : In a large bowl, combine the masa harina, milk, softened butter, sugar, vanilla, baking powder, salt, and optional cinnamon. Mix until the dough is smooth and well combined.
3. **Blend the corn** : In a blender or food processor, blend the fresh or thawed corn kernels until smooth, with a few whole kernels left for texture. If needed, add a little water to help blend.
4. **Combine corn with masa** : Add the blended corn mixture to the masa dough and stir until fully incorporated. The dough should be moist but firm.
5. **Assemble the tamales** : Take one corn husk and spread a small amount of masa mixture (about 2 tablespoons) in the center, leaving space at the edges. Fold in the sides of the husk, then fold up the bottom to enclose the tamale. Repeat with the remaining husks and masa.
6. **Steam the tamales** : Place the tamales standing up in a large steamer. Cover the top with a clean cloth, then steam for 1 hour to 1 hour 30 minutes, or until the masa pulls away from the husk. Check the water level in the steamer occasionally and add more water if needed.
7. **Serve and enjoy** : Let the tamales cool for a few minutes before serving. Enjoy your sweet tamales with a cup of hot coffee or a refreshing agua fresca!

Soups & Comfort Bowls

Servings: 4 | Prep Time: 15 minutes | Cook Time: 30 minutes

~400 kcal per serving

Ingredients:

- 1 tbsp (15 ml) olive oil
- 1 small onion, finely chopped
- 2 garlic cloves, minced
- 1 cup (240 g) chopped tomatoes
- 4 cups (1 L) vegetable or chicken broth
- 1 cup (200 g) corn kernels (fresh or frozen)
- 1 1/2 cups (200 g) cooked shredded chicken (optional)
- 1/2 cup (80 g) cooked rice (optional)
- 1 tsp (5 g) ground cumin
- 1 tsp (5 g) chili powder
- Salt and pepper to taste
- 1/2 cup (120 ml) fresh lime juice
- 1/4 cup (30 g) fresh cilantro, chopped
- [Optional] 1/2 avocado, sliced for garnish
- [Optional] Crumbled tortilla chips for garnish

Instructions:

1. **Sauté the aromatics** : In a large pot, heat the olive oil over medium heat. Add the chopped onion and cook until softened, about 5 minutes. Add the minced garlic and cook for another minute, until fragrant.
2. **Add the tomatoes and spices** : Stir in the chopped tomatoes, cumin, and chili powder. Cook for 2-3 minutes, allowing the tomatoes to break down and release their juices.
3. **Add the broth and corn** : Pour in the vegetable or chicken broth and add the corn kernels. Stir to combine and bring the soup to a simmer.
4. **Simmer and season** : Let the soup simmer for 15-20 minutes, until the flavors meld together. If you're using cooked shredded chicken and rice, add them now and continue simmering for another 5 minutes.
5. **Finish with lime and cilantro** : Remove the soup from the heat and stir in the fresh lime juice and chopped cilantro. Taste and adjust seasoning with salt and pepper.
6. **Serve and garnish** : Ladle the soup into bowls and garnish with slices of avocado and crumbled tortilla chips, if desired. Enjoy a comforting, flavorful bowl of Mexican-style soup!

Black Bean Soup with Lime

Servings: 4 | Prep Time: 10 minutes | Cook Time: 25 minutes

~350 kcal per serving

Ingredients:

- 1 tbsp (15 ml) olive oil
- 1 small onion, chopped
- 2 garlic cloves, minced
- 1 (15 oz / 425 g) can black beans, drained and rinsed
- 4 cups (1 L) vegetable broth
- 1 tsp (5 g) ground cumin
- 1 tsp (5 g) chili powder
- Salt and pepper to taste
- 1/2 tsp (2 g) smoked paprika
- Juice of 1 lime
- [Optional] 1/2 cup (120 ml) sour cream or Greek yogurt for creaminess
- [Optional] Fresh cilantro for garnish
- [Optional] Crumbled tortilla chips for garnish

Instructions:

1. **Sauté the aromatics** : Heat the olive oil in a large pot over medium heat. Add the chopped onion and cook for 5 minutes, or until softened. Add the minced garlic and cook for another minute, until fragrant.
2. **Add the black beans and spices** : Stir in the black beans, ground cumin, chili powder, smoked paprika, salt, and pepper. Cook for 2-3 minutes, allowing the spices to bloom.
3. **Add the broth** : Pour in the vegetable broth and bring the soup to a boil. Reduce the heat to a simmer and cook for 15-20 minutes, allowing the flavors to meld.
4. **Blend the soup** : For a creamier texture, use an immersion blender to purée the soup slightly. Alternatively, you can transfer half of the soup to a blender, purée, and return it to the pot.
5. **Finish with lime** : Stir in the fresh lime juice for a bright, zesty flavor. Taste and adjust seasoning as needed.
6. **Serve and garnish** : Ladle the soup into bowls. Optionally, add a dollop of sour cream or Greek yogurt for creaminess. Garnish with fresh cilantro and crumbled tortilla chips for a delicious crunch.

Mexican Chicken Soup (Caldo de Pollo)

Servings: 6 | Prep Time: 15 minutes | Cook Time: 45 minutes

~**400** kcal per serving

Ingredients:

- 1 tbsp (15 ml) olive oil
- 1 medium onion, chopped
- 2 garlic cloves, minced
- 1 (3 lb / 1.4 kg) whole chicken, cut into pieces
- 10 cups (2.4 L) chicken broth
- 2 medium carrots, peeled and sliced
- 2 medium potatoes, peeled and cubed
- 2 medium zucchini, chopped
- 1 cup (150 g) corn kernels
- 2 bay leaves
- 1 tsp (5 g) ground cumin
- 1 tsp (5 g) dried oregano
- Salt and pepper to taste
- Juice of 1 lime
- [Optional] Fresh cilantro for garnish
- [Optional] Tortilla strips for garnish

Instructions:

1. **Sauté the aromatics**: Heat the olive oil in a large pot over medium heat. Add the chopped onion and cook for 5 minutes, or until softened. Stir in the minced garlic and cook for another minute, until fragrant.
2. **Cook the chicken**: Add the chicken pieces to the pot and brown them slightly on all sides, about 5 minutes.
3. **Add the broth and vegetables**: Pour in the chicken broth and bring to a boil. Add the carrots, potatoes, zucchini, corn, bay leaves, cumin, and oregano.
4. **Simmer the soup**: Reduce the heat to low and let the soup simmer for 30-40 minutes, or until the chicken is cooked through and the vegetables are tender.
5. **Season the soup**: Remove the chicken pieces from the pot, shred the meat, and return it to the soup. Season with salt, pepper, and lime juice to taste.
6. **Serve and garnish**: Ladle the soup into bowls. Optionally, garnish with fresh cilantro and tortilla strips for a traditional touch.

Pozole Rojo (Simplified Version)

~350 kcal per serving

Servings: 6 | Prep Time: 15 minutes | Cook Time: 1 hour

Ingredients:

- 2 tbsp (30 ml) olive oil
- 1 lb (450 g) pork shoulder, cut into chunks
- 1 medium onion, chopped
- 3 garlic cloves, minced
- 2 tbsp (30 g) red chile powder
- 1 tsp (5 g) ground cumin
- 1 (15 oz / 425 g) can hominy, drained and rinsed
- 6 cups (1.4 L) chicken broth
- 1 (14 oz / 400 g) can diced tomatoes
- Salt and pepper to taste
- Juice of 1 lime
- [Optional] Sliced radishes for garnish
- [Optional] Fresh cilantro for garnish
- [Optional] Tortilla strips for garnish

Instructions:

1. **Sauté the pork** : Heat the olive oil in a large pot over medium heat. Add the pork shoulder chunks and brown on all sides, about 5-7 minutes.
2. **Cook the aromatics** : Add the chopped onion and minced garlic to the pot. Cook for 3-4 minutes until softened.
3. **Season the soup** : Stir in the red chile powder and ground cumin, cooking for 1-2 minutes to bring out the flavors.
4. **Add the liquids and hominy** : Pour in the chicken broth and diced tomatoes. Stir to combine, then add the hominy. Bring the mixture to a boil.
5. **Simmer the soup** : Reduce the heat to low and let the soup simmer for 45 minutes, or until the pork is tender and fully cooked.
6. **Season and finish** : Add salt, pepper, and lime juice to taste.
7. **Serve and garnish** : Ladle the soup into bowls and garnish with sliced radishes, fresh cilantro, and tortilla strips, if desired.

Albondigas Soup (Mexican Meatball Soup)

Servings: 6 | Prep Time: 20 minutes | Cook Time: 45 minutes

~300 kcal per serving

Ingredients:

- 1 lb (450 g) ground beef
- 1/2 cup (75 g) cooked rice
- 1/4 cup (25 g) breadcrumbs
- 1 egg
- 2 tbsp (30 ml) chopped fresh cilantro
- 1 tsp (5 g) ground cumin
- 1/2 tsp (2 g) dried oregano
- 1/2 tsp (2 g) garlic powder
- 1/2 tsp (2 g) onion powder
- Salt and pepper to taste
- 1 tbsp (15 ml) olive oil
- 1 small onion, chopped
- 2 garlic cloves, minced
- 1 (14 oz / 400 g) can diced tomatoes
- 6 cups (1.4 L) chicken broth
- 2 medium carrots, peeled and sliced
- 2 medium potatoes, peeled and diced
- [Optional] Fresh cilantro for garnish
- [Optional] Lime wedges for serving

Instructions:

1. **Prepare the meatballs**: In a large mixing bowl, combine the ground beef, cooked rice, breadcrumbs, egg, cilantro, cumin, oregano, garlic powder, onion powder, salt, and pepper. Mix well until all ingredients are evenly incorporated. Form the mixture into small meatballs, about 1-inch in diameter. Set aside.
2. **Sauté the aromatics**: Heat the olive oil in a large pot over medium heat. Add the chopped onion and minced garlic. Sauté for 3-4 minutes, until softened and fragrant.
3. **Cook the soup base**: Add the diced tomatoes (with juices) and chicken broth to the pot. Stir to combine and bring the mixture to a boil.
4. **Simmer the meatballs**: Gently add the meatballs to the pot, one by one, ensuring they are submerged in the broth. Reduce the heat to low and simmer for 20-25 minutes, or until the meatballs are cooked through.
5. **Add the vegetables**: Add the sliced carrots and diced potatoes to the soup. Continue to simmer for an additional 15-20 minutes, or until the vegetables are tender.
6. **Season the soup**: Taste the soup and adjust the seasoning with salt and pepper as needed.
7. **Serve and garnish**: Ladle the soup into bowls. Garnish with fresh cilantro and serve with lime wedges on the side for a refreshing burst of flavor.

Mexican Rice Soup

Servings: 6 | Prep Time: 10 minutes | Cook Time: 30 minutes

Ingredients:

- 1 cup (200 g) long-grain white rice
- 1 tbsp (15 ml) olive oil
- 1 small onion, chopped
- 2 garlic cloves, minced
- 1 (14 oz / 400 g) can diced tomatoes
- 4 cups (1 L) chicken or vegetable broth
- 1 carrot, peeled and diced
- 1 zucchini, diced
- 1/2 tsp (2 g) ground cumin
- 1/4 tsp (1 g) chili powder
- Salt and pepper to taste
- 1 tbsp (15 ml) fresh lime juice
- [Optional] Fresh cilantro for garnish
- [Optional] Tortilla chips or strips for garnish

Instructions:

1. **Toast the rice** : In a large pot, heat the olive oil over medium heat. Add the rice and sauté for 2-3 minutes until the rice is lightly golden and fragrant.
2. **Sauté the aromatics** : Add the chopped onion and minced garlic to the pot. Cook for another 2-3 minutes, stirring occasionally, until the onion becomes translucent.
3. **Add the tomatoes and broth** : Stir in the diced tomatoes (with juices) and chicken or vegetable broth. Bring the mixture to a boil.
4. **Cook the vegetables** : Add the diced carrot and zucchini to the pot. Reduce the heat to low and let the soup simmer for 15-20 minutes, or until the rice is tender and the vegetables are cooked through.
5. **Season the soup** : Stir in the cumin, chili powder, salt, and pepper to taste. Add the lime juice and adjust seasoning if necessary.
6. **Serve and garnish** : Ladle the soup into bowls and garnish with fresh cilantro and tortilla chips or strips if desired.

Frijoles de la Olla (Simple Stewed Beans)

Servings: 6 | Prep Time: 10 minutes | Cook Time: 1 hour 30 minutes

Ingredients:

- 2 cups (400 g) dried pinto beans
- 8 cups (2 L) water
- 1 small onion, peeled
- 2 garlic cloves, smashed
- 1 bay leaf
- 1 tsp (5 g) salt
- [Optional] 1 tbsp (15 ml) olive oil or lard
- [Optional] 1/2 tsp (2 g) ground cumin or chili powder

Instructions:

1. **Rinse the beans** : Rinse the dried pinto beans thoroughly under cold water to remove any dirt or debris.
2. **Cook the beans** : In a large pot, add the rinsed beans and 8 cups of water. Bring to a boil over medium-high heat.
3. **Add aromatics** : Once the water is boiling, add the onion, garlic, and bay leaf. Reduce the heat to low, cover the pot, and simmer for about 1 hour, or until the beans are tender.
4. **Season the beans** : After the beans are tender, add the salt and stir. For added flavor, you can also include olive oil or lard, as well as ground cumin or chili powder if desired.
5. **Serve** : Remove the onion, garlic, and bay leaf before serving. Ladle the beans into bowls and enjoy them as a side dish or part of your favorite tortilla soup.

Chicken and Hominy Soup (Caldo de Maíz)

~220 kcal per serving

Servings: 6 | Prep Time: 10 minutes | Cook Time: 1 hour 15 minutes

Ingredients:

- 1 lb (450 g) chicken thighs or breasts, bone-in
- 8 cups (2 L) water
- 1 can (15 oz or 425 g) hominy, drained and rinsed
- 2 medium tomatoes, diced
- 1 medium onion, chopped
- 2 garlic cloves, minced
- 2 carrots, peeled and sliced
- 1 tsp (5 g) salt, or to taste
- 1/2 tsp (2 g) ground black pepper
- 2 tbsp (30 ml) vegetable oil or olive oil
- [Optional] 1-2 jalapeños, chopped (for heat)
- [Optional] Fresh cilantro, chopped (for garnish)

Instructions:

1. **Cook the chicken** : In a large pot, add the chicken thighs or breasts along with 8 cups of water. Bring to a boil over medium-high heat. Once boiling, reduce the heat and simmer for about 30 minutes until the chicken is cooked through.
2. **Prepare the soup base** : While the chicken cooks, heat the oil in a skillet over medium heat. Add the chopped onion, garlic, and diced tomatoes. Cook for about 5 minutes, until the onions are soft and the tomatoes have broken down. If you want extra heat, add the chopped jalapeños at this stage.
3. **Add the vegetables and hominy** : After the chicken is cooked, remove it from the pot and set aside to cool. Add the sliced carrots, hominy, and the sautéed onion-tomato mixture to the broth. Stir well and let it simmer for another 15 minutes.
4. **Shred the chicken** : Once the chicken is cool enough to handle, remove the bones and shred the meat. Return the shredded chicken to the pot.
5. **Season and finish** : Season the soup with salt and pepper to taste. Let the soup simmer for another 10 minutes to allow all the flavors to meld together.
6. **Serve** : Ladle the soup into bowls and garnish with fresh cilantro, if desired. Serve hot with a side of tortillas or a squeeze of lime.

Sopa de Fideo (Mexican Vermicelli Soup)

~180 kcal per serving

Servings: 4 | Prep Time: 10 minutes | Cook Time: 20 minutes

Ingredients:

- 2 tbsp (30 ml) vegetable oil
- 4 oz (115 g) fideo noodles (vermicelli noodles)
- 1 medium onion, chopped
- 2 garlic cloves, minced
- 2 medium tomatoes, diced
- 4 cups (1 L) chicken or vegetable broth
- 1 tsp (5 g) salt, or to taste
- 1/2 tsp (2 g) ground black pepper
- 1/2 tsp (2 g) ground cumin
- 1/4 tsp (1 g) ground chili powder
- 1/4 tsp (1 g) dried oregano
- 1/2 cup (75 g) frozen peas (optional)
- [Optional] Fresh cilantro, chopped (for garnish)
- [Optional] Lime wedges (for serving)

Instructions:

1. **Toast the noodles**: In a large pot, heat the vegetable oil over medium heat. Add the fideo noodles and sauté for 3–5 minutes, stirring occasionally, until they are lightly golden brown. Be careful not to burn them.
2. **Prepare the soup base**: Add the chopped onion and garlic to the pot. Sauté for another 2–3 minutes until the onion softens and becomes translucent.
3. **Cook the tomatoes**: Stir in the diced tomatoes, salt, pepper, cumin, chili powder, and oregano. Cook for 5 minutes, allowing the tomatoes to break down and the spices to become fragrant.
4. **Add the broth**: Pour in the chicken or vegetable broth and bring the mixture to a boil. Once boiling, reduce the heat and simmer for about 10 minutes to let the flavors meld together.
5. **Cook the noodles**: Add the frozen peas (if using) and stir in the toasted fideo noodles. Let the soup simmer for an additional 5 minutes, or until the noodles are cooked through and tender.
6. **Serve**: Ladle the soup into bowls and garnish with fresh cilantro, if desired. Serve with a wedge of lime for a zesty touch.

Ground Beef Tacos

Servings: 4 | Prep Time: 10 minutes | Cook Time: 15 minutes

~250 kcal per serving

Ingredients:

- 1 lb (450 g) ground beef
- 1 tbsp (15 ml) vegetable oil
- 1 medium onion, finely chopped
- 2 garlic cloves, minced
- Homemade Taco Seasoning (makes ~1 oz)
  - 1 tsp chili powder
  - 1/2 tsp ground cumin
  - 1/2 tsp smoked paprika
  - 1/4 tsp garlic powder
  - 1/4 tsp onion powder
  - 1/4 tsp dried oregano
  - 1/4 tsp salt
- 1/2 cup (120 ml) water
- 1 tbsp (15 ml) tomato paste
- 8 small soft corn or flour tortillas
- 1 cup (150 g) shredded lettuce
- 1/2 cup (75 g) diced tomatoes
- 1/4 cup (30 g) shredded cheddar cheese
- 1/4 cup (30 g) sour cream
- [Optional] Fresh cilantro, chopped (for garnish)
- [Optional] Salsa or hot sauce (for serving)

Instructions:

1. **Cook the beef**: In a large skillet, heat the vegetable oil over medium-high heat. Add the ground beef and cook, breaking it up with a spoon, until browned and fully cooked (about 5–7 minutes). Drain any excess fat if necessary.
2. **Add the seasonings**: Add the chopped onion and minced garlic to the skillet with the beef. Sauté for 2–3 minutes until softened.
3. **Season the beef**: Stir in the *homemade taco seasoning*, water, and tomato paste. Bring the mixture to a simmer, then cook for 3–4 minutes, or until the sauce thickens and the flavors combine.
4. **Warm the tortillas:** While the beef is simmering, warm the tortillas in a dry skillet over medium heat for about 1 minute per side, or until soft and slightly charred.
5. **Assemble the tacos**: Spoon the seasoned ground beef mixture onto the center of each tortilla. Top with shredded lettuce, diced tomatoes, and shredded cheddar cheese. Add sour cream, cilantro, or salsa if desired.

Chicken Tinga Tacos

~280 kcal per serving

Servings: 4 | Prep Time: 10 minutes | Cook Time: 25 minutes

Ingredients:

- 1 lb (450 g) boneless, skinless chicken breasts
- 1 tbsp (15 ml) vegetable oil
- 1 medium onion, thinly sliced
- 2 garlic cloves, minced
- 2 chipotle peppers in adobo sauce, chopped
- 1/4 cup (60 ml) adobo sauce (from the chipotle can)
- 1 tsp (5 g) ground cumin
- 1 tsp (5 g) smoked paprika
- 1/2 tsp (2 g) dried oregano
- 1/2 tsp (2 g) salt (or to taste)
- 1/4 tsp (1 g) black pepper
- 1 cup (240 ml) chicken broth
- 8 small soft corn or flour tortillas
- 1 cup (150 g) shredded lettuce
- 1/2 cup (75 g) diced tomatoes
- 1/4 cup (30 g) crumbled queso fresco
- [Optional] Fresh cilantro, chopped (for garnish)
- [Optional] Lime wedges (for serving)

Instructions:

1. **Cook the chicken** : In a large pot, add the chicken breasts and enough water to cover. Bring to a boil, then lower the heat and simmer for 15–20 minutes, or until the chicken is fully cooked and tender. Once done, shred the chicken using two forks and set it aside.
2. **Prepare the tinga sauce** : In a skillet, heat the vegetable oil over medium heat. Add the sliced onion and garlic, and sauté for 3–4 minutes, until softened and fragrant.
3. **Add the seasonings** : Stir in the chopped chipotle peppers, adobo sauce, ground cumin, smoked paprika, oregano, salt, and black pepper. Cook for 2–3 minutes, letting the flavors meld together.
4. **Simmer the chicken** : Add the shredded chicken to the skillet with the sauce, then pour in the chicken broth. Stir to combine and let the mixture simmer for 5–7 minutes, or until the sauce thickens slightly.
5. **Warm the tortillas** : While the chicken is simmering, warm the tortillas in a dry skillet over medium heat for 1–2 minutes per side until soft and slightly charred.
6. **Assemble the tacos** : Spoon the chicken tinga mixture onto the center of each tortilla. Top with shredded lettuce, diced tomatoes, and crumbled queso fresco.
7. **Serve** : Garnish with fresh cilantro and serve with lime wedges on the side for a burst of freshness.

Baja Fish Tacos

~320 kcal per serving

Servings: 4 | Prep Time: 15 minutes | Cook Time: 10 minutes

Ingredients:

- 1 lb (450 g) firm white fish fillets (such as cod or tilapia)
- 1/2 cup (60 g) all-purpose flour
- 1/2 tsp (2 g) ground cumin
- 1/2 tsp (2 g) chili powder
- 1/4 tsp (1 g) garlic powder
- 1/4 tsp (1 g) salt
- 1/4 tsp (1 g) black pepper
- 1 large egg
- 1/2 cup (120 ml) cold beer (or use sparkling water for a non-alcoholic version)
- Vegetable oil (for frying)
- 8 small corn tortillas
- 1 cup (150 g) shredded cabbage
- 1/2 cup (75 g) diced tomatoes
- 1/4 cup (60 g) chopped fresh cilantro
- 1/4 cup (60 ml) sour cream
- 1 tbsp (15 ml) lime juice
- 1 tsp (5 g) hot sauce (optional, for extra heat)
- [Optional] Lime wedges (for serving)

Instructions:

1. **Prepare the fish**: Pat the fish fillets dry with paper towels. Cut the fish into strips, about 1–2 inches wide.
2. **Make the batter**: In a shallow bowl, whisk together the flour, cumin, chili powder, garlic powder, salt, and pepper. In another bowl, beat the egg and then whisk in the cold beer (or sparkling water) to create a batter.
3. **Coat the fish**: Dip each piece of fish into the batter, ensuring it is fully coated.
4. **Fry the fish**: Heat about 1 inch of vegetable oil in a large skillet over medium-high heat. Once the oil is hot (you can test it by dropping a small amount of batter into the oil; it should sizzle immediately), fry the fish in batches for 2–3 minutes per side, or until golden brown and crispy. Remove the fish from the oil and drain on a paper towel-lined plate.
5. **Warm the tortillas**: While the fish is cooking, warm the tortillas in a dry skillet over medium heat for 1–2 minutes per side until soft and slightly charred.
6. **Prepare the creamy sauce**: In a small bowl, mix together the sour cream, lime juice, and hot sauce (if using). Adjust to taste.
7. **Assemble the tacos**: Place a few pieces of fried fish onto each tortilla. Top with shredded cabbage, diced tomatoes, and fresh cilantro. Drizzle with the creamy sauce.

Shrimp Tacos with Garlic Lime Sauce

~350 kcal per serving

Servings: 4 | Prep Time: 15 minutes | Cook Time: 10 minutes

Ingredients:

- 1 lb (450 g) large shrimp, peeled and deveined
- 1 tbsp (15 ml) olive oil
- 1/2 tsp (2 g) ground cumin
- 1/4 tsp (1 g) chili powder
- 1/4 tsp (1 g) smoked paprika
- 1/4 tsp (1 g) salt
- 1/4 tsp (1 g) black pepper
- 1 tbsp (15 ml) lime juice
- 8 small corn tortillas
- 1 cup (150 g) shredded cabbage
- 1/2 cup (75 g) diced tomatoes
- 1/4 cup (60 g) chopped fresh cilantro

For the Garlic Lime Sauce

- 3 tbsp (45 g) mayonnaise
- 1 tbsp (15 ml) lime juice
- 2 cloves garlic, minced
- 1 tsp (5 ml) hot sauce (optional, for extra heat)

Instructions:

1. **Prepare the shrimp**: In a medium bowl, toss the shrimp with olive oil, cumin, chili powder, smoked paprika, salt, and pepper. Let it marinate for about 5 minutes to absorb the flavors.
2. **Make the garlic lime sauce**: In a small bowl, whisk together the mayonnaise, lime juice, minced garlic, and hot sauce (if using). Set aside.
3. **Cook the shrimp**: Heat a large skillet over medium-high heat. Once hot, add the shrimp and cook for 2-3 minutes per side, or until they turn pink and are cooked through.
4. **Warm the tortillas**: While the shrimp is cooking, warm the tortillas in a dry skillet over medium heat for 1-2 minutes per side until soft and slightly charred.
5. **Assemble the tacos**: Place a few shrimp on each tortilla. Top with shredded cabbage, diced tomatoes, and fresh cilantro.
6. **Drizzle the sauce**: Spoon the garlic lime sauce over the shrimp and toppings, ensuring each taco is generously coated.
7. **Serve**: Garnish with extra lime wedges for added flavor and enjoy your delicious, zesty Shrimp Tacos with Garlic Lime Sauce.

Elote (Mexican Street Corn)

Servings: 4 | Prep Time: 5 minutes | Cook Time: 10 minutes

~290 kcal per serving

Ingredients:

- 4 ears of corn, husked
- 2 tbsp (30 g) butter, melted
- 1/4 cup (60 g) mayonnaise
- 1/4 cup (25 g) crumbled cotija cheese
- 1 tbsp (15 ml) lime juice
- 1/2 tsp (2 g) chili powder
- 1/4 tsp (1 g) smoked paprika
- 1/4 tsp (1 g) garlic powder
- [Optional] Fresh cilantro, chopped, for garnish
- [Optional] Lime wedges for serving

Instructions:

1. **Grill the corn** : Preheat your grill to medium-high heat. Place the husked corn directly on the grill and cook for 8-10 minutes, turning occasionally, until the corn is tender and slightly charred on all sides.
2. **Prepare the sauce** : While the corn is grilling, mix the melted butter, mayonnaise, lime juice, chili powder, smoked paprika, and garlic powder in a small bowl.
3. **Coat the corn** : Once the corn is grilled, remove it from the heat and immediately brush each ear with the prepared sauce, making sure the corn is evenly coated.
4. **Add the toppings** : Sprinkle the crumbled cotija cheese over the coated corn, ensuring each ear has a generous layer.
5. **Garnish and serve** : Optionally, sprinkle with fresh cilantro for an extra burst of flavor, and serve with lime wedges for squeezing over the top.

Nachos with Pico de Gallo and Cheese Sauce

Servings: 4 | Prep Time: 10 minutes | Cook Time: 5 minutes

~450 kcal per serving

Ingredients:

- 8 oz (225 g) tortilla chips
- 1 cup (150 g) shredded cheddar cheese
- 1/2 cup (120 ml) milk
- 2 tbsp (30 g) butter
- 2 tbsp (30 g) all-purpose flour
- 1/4 tsp (1 g) garlic powder
- 1/4 tsp (1 g) onion powder
- 1/4 tsp (1 g) chili powder
- 1 tbsp (15 ml) lime juice
- 1 cup (150 g) fresh pico de gallo (see instructions for preparation)
- [Optional] Jalapeño slices for garnish
- [Optional] Fresh cilantro for garnish

Instructions:

1. **Prepare the cheese sauce**: In a small saucepan, melt the butter over medium heat. Once melted, whisk in the flour, garlic powder, onion powder, and chili powder. Cook for 1-2 minutes, stirring constantly.
2. **Make the cheese sauce**: Gradually add the milk to the mixture while stirring to avoid lumps. Continue to cook for 2-3 minutes until the sauce thickens. Lower the heat and stir in the shredded cheddar cheese until completely melted and smooth. Set aside.
3. **Prepare the pico de gallo**: In a small bowl, combine **1 cup diced tomatoes**, **1/4 cup diced onions**, **1/4 cup chopped cilantro**, and **1-2 tbsp lime juice**. Season with salt and pepper to taste.
4. **Assemble the nachos**: Spread the tortilla chips evenly on a serving platter. Drizzle the warm cheese sauce over the chips, ensuring they are well covered.
5. **Top with pico de gallo**: Spoon the pico de gallo generously over the nachos.
6. **Garnish and serve**: For extra flavor, garnish with optional jalapeño slices and fresh cilantro. Serve immediately while the nachos are warm and the cheese sauce is gooey!

Queso Fundido with Chorizo

~350 kcal per serving

Servings: 4 | Prep Time: 5 minutes | Cook Time: 10 minutes

Ingredients:

- 1 lb (450 g) Mexican chorizo
- 8 oz (225 g) Oaxaca cheese, shredded
- 8 oz (225 g) mozzarella cheese, shredded
- 1/4 cup (60 ml) milk
- 1 tbsp (15 g) butter
- [Optional] 1/4 cup (60 g) diced onions
- [Optional] 1 tbsp (15 g) chopped fresh cilantro
- Corn or flour tortillas for serving

Instructions:

1. **Cook the chorizo** : Heat a skillet over medium heat. Add the chorizo (remove from casing if necessary) and cook for 5-7 minutes, breaking it up with a spoon until browned and fully cooked. If using, add the diced onions and cook for an additional 2 minutes until softened.
2. **Prepare the cheese mixture** : In a separate saucepan, melt the butter over medium heat. Add the shredded Oaxaca and mozzarella cheese along with the milk. Stir continuously until the cheese is completely melted and smooth.
3. **Combine** : Add the cooked chorizo (and onions, if using) to the melted cheese mixture, stirring to combine evenly. Cook for an additional 1-2 minutes, allowing the flavors to meld together.
4. **Serve** : Transfer the queso fundido to a serving dish, and sprinkle with optional chopped cilantro for a fresh, herby touch.
5. **Enjoy** : Serve with warm corn or flour tortillas for dipping. Enjoy your indulgent, melty Queso Fundido with Chorizo!

Gorditas with Refried Beans

Servings: 4 | Prep Time: 10 minutes | Cook Time: 15 minutes

~290 kcal per serving

Ingredients:

- 2 cups (250 g) masa harina
- 1/2 tsp salt
- 1 tsp baking powder
- 1 tbsp (15 ml) vegetable oil
- 1 cup (240 ml) warm water
- 1 cup (240 g) refried beans
- [Optional] 1/4 cup (60 g) crumbled queso fresco
- [Optional] 1/4 cup (60 g) salsa for serving

Instructions:

1. **Make the dough**: In a large bowl, combine the masa harina, salt, and baking powder. Add the vegetable oil and warm water, mixing until a smooth dough forms. If the dough feels too dry, add a little more water, one tablespoon at a time.
2. **Form the gorditas**: Divide the dough into 8 equal portions. Roll each portion into a ball, then flatten each ball into a thick disk, about 1/2 inch (1.25 cm) thick.
3. **Cook the gorditas**: Heat a large skillet or griddle over medium heat. Place the gorditas in the pan and cook for 3-4 minutes per side, or until golden brown and slightly puffed. You may need to press down lightly on the gorditas with a spatula to ensure even cooking.
4. **Fill with refried beans**: Once the gorditas are cooked, cut a slit along the side of each one, creating a pocket. Spoon in the refried beans, filling them generously.
5. **Optional toppings**: For extra flavor, sprinkle with crumbled queso fresco or serve with salsa on the side.
6. **Serve and enjoy**: Serve the Gorditas with Refried Beans hot, as a satisfying snack or a meal on the go!

Sopes with Chicken or Veggies

~350 kcal per serving

Servings: 4 | Prep Time: 15 minutes | Cook Time: 20 minutes

Ingredients:

- 2 cups (250 g) masa harina
- 1/2 tsp salt
- 1 tsp baking powder
- 1 tbsp (15 ml) vegetable oil
- 1/2 cup (120 ml) warm water
- 1 lb (450 g) cooked chicken, shredded
- 1 cup (150 g) mixed veggies (e.g., bell peppers, zucchini, mushrooms), sautéed
- 1/2 cup (75 g) refried beans
- 1/4 cup (60 g) Mexican crema
- 1/2 cup (60 g) lettuce, finely shredded
- 1/4 cup (60 g) crumbled queso fresco
- 1/4 cup (60 ml) salsa (optional)
- [Optional] 1 tbsp chopped cilantro

Instructions:

1. **Prepare the dough**: In a large bowl, mix the masa harina, salt, and baking powder. Add the vegetable oil and warm water, stirring until a smooth dough forms. If the dough is too dry, add a little more water, one tablespoon at a time.
2. **Shape the sopes**: Divide the dough into 8 equal portions. Roll each portion into a ball, then flatten each ball into a thick disk, about 1/2 inch (1.25 cm) thick. Pinch the edges to create a raised border.
3. **Cook the sopes**: Heat a skillet over medium heat. Cook the sopes in the hot skillet for 3-4 minutes per side, or until they're golden brown and slightly crispy.
4. **Prepare the filling**: While the sopes cook, heat the refried beans in a small pan. You can also warm the shredded chicken or sautéed veggies.
5. **Assemble the sopes**: Once the sopes are cooked, spread a thin layer of refried beans on each one. Top with shredded chicken or sautéed veggies, depending on your choice.
6. **Add toppings**: Drizzle with Mexican crema, then sprinkle with shredded lettuce, crumbled queso fresco, and chopped cilantro (if desired).
7. **Serve with salsa**: For extra flavor, serve with salsa on the side.
8. **Enjoy**: Serve your **Sopes with Chicken or Veggies** hot, as a delicious snack or meal.

Chicken Flautas (Crispy Rolled Tacos)

Servings: 4 | Prep Time: 15 minutes | Cook Time: 20 minutes

~450 kcal per serving

Ingredients:

- 2 cups (300 g) cooked chicken, shredded
- 1/2 cup (80 g) diced onion
- 1/2 cup (80 g) diced tomato
- 1/2 cup (120 g) shredded cheese (Mexican blend or Oaxaca)
- 1/4 cup (60 ml) chicken broth
- 1 tsp cumin
- 1/2 tsp garlic powder
- 1/4 tsp chili powder
- 1/4 tsp black pepper
- 8 small corn tortillas
- Vegetable oil, for frying
- [Optional] 1/4 cup (60 g) salsa
- [Optional] 1/4 cup (60 g) sour cream
- [Optional] Fresh cilantro, chopped, for garnish

Instructions:

1. **Prepare the filling**: In a bowl, combine the shredded chicken, diced onion, diced tomato, shredded cheese, chicken broth, cumin, garlic powder, chili powder, and black pepper. Mix well to combine.
2. **Warm the tortillas**: Heat the tortillas in a dry skillet or microwave for a few seconds to soften them. This will make them easier to roll.
3. **Fill the tortillas**: Spoon a generous amount of the chicken mixture onto the center of each tortilla. Roll up the tortillas tightly, ensuring the ends are tucked in so the filling doesn't spill out.
4. **Fry the flautas**: Heat about 1 inch of vegetable oil in a skillet over medium heat. Once the oil is hot (about 350°F or 175°C), carefully place the rolled tortillas seam-side down into the oil. Fry for 3-4 minutes per side or until golden and crispy.
5. **Drain the excess oil**: Remove the flautas from the oil and place them on a plate lined with paper towels to drain any excess oil.
6. **Serve**: Arrange the crispy chicken flautas on a plate. Optionally, drizzle with salsa or sour cream and garnish with fresh cilantro.
7. **Enjoy**: Serve hot, with extra salsa or crema on the side for dipping.

Mexican Street Tostadas

~350 kcal
per serving

Servings: 4 | Prep Time: 15 minutes | Cook Time: 10 minutes

Ingredients:

- 4 tostada shells (store-bought or homemade)
- 1 cup (200 g) cooked and shredded chicken, beef, or beans (choose your preferred protein)
- 1/2 cup (80 g) refried beans (optional, for a heartier base)
- 1/2 cup (80 g) shredded lettuce
- 1/4 cup (40 g) diced tomato
- 1/4 cup (40 g) diced onion
- 1/4 cup (60 g) crumbled queso fresco
- 1/4 cup (60 ml) sour cream
- 1/4 cup (60 g) salsa or pico de gallo
- 1 tbsp (15 ml) lime juice
- 1/4 tsp (1 g) chili powder
- 1/4 tsp (1 g) cumin
- Salt and pepper, to taste
- [Optional] Fresh cilantro, chopped, for garnish

Instructions:

1. **Prepare the toppings** : In a small bowl, combine the diced tomato, diced onion, and a squeeze of lime juice. Season with a pinch of salt, pepper, chili powder, and cumin. Mix well and set aside.
2. **Warm the tostada shells** : If using store-bought tostada shells, heat them in a dry skillet over medium heat for 1-2 minutes per side, or until they become crispy and slightly golden.
3. **Assemble the tostadas** : Spread a thin layer of refried beans on each tostada shell, if using. Add a generous portion of your protein (shredded chicken, beef, or beans) on top.
4. **Add the fresh toppings** : Top the tostada with shredded lettuce, the tomato-onion mixture, and crumbled queso fresco.
5. **Drizzle with sour cream and salsa** : Add a spoonful of sour cream and a dollop of salsa or pico de gallo on top of each tostada.
6. **Garnish and serve** : Sprinkle with chopped fresh cilantro, if desired, and serve immediately.
7. **Enjoy** : Enjoy these crunchy, flavorful Mexican Street Tostadas as a snack, appetizer, or light meal.

Carne Asada (Grilled Beef)

Servings: 4 | Prep Time: 15 minutes | Cook Time: 10 minutes

~450 kcal per serving

Ingredients:

- 1 lb (450 g) flank steak or skirt steak
- 3 tbsp (45 ml) olive oil
- 2 tbsp (30 ml) lime juice
- 3 cloves garlic, minced
- 1 tsp (5 g) ground cumin
- 1 tsp (5 g) chili powder
- 1/2 tsp (2 g) ground black pepper
- 1/2 tsp (2 g) paprika
- 1/4 tsp (1 g) ground oregano
- 1/4 tsp (1 g) ground coriander
- Salt, to taste
- [Optional] 1 jalapeño, minced (for extra heat)
- 1/4 cup (60 g) chopped fresh cilantro
- 1 tbsp (15 ml) orange juice (optional, for extra flavor)

Instructions:

1. **Marinate the steak**: In a large bowl, combine the olive oil, lime juice, minced garlic, cumin, chili powder, black pepper, paprika, oregano, coriander, and salt. Add the jalapeño if you prefer a bit of heat. Mix well to form the marinade.
2. **Coat the steak**: Place the flank or skirt steak in the marinade, making sure it is evenly coated. Cover and refrigerate for at least 30 minutes (or up to 2 hours) to allow the flavors to meld.
3. **Preheat the grill**: Heat a grill or grill pan over medium-high heat. Lightly oil the grates or pan to prevent sticking.
4. **Grill the steak**: Remove the steak from the marinade and grill it for about 4-5 minutes per side for medium-rare, or longer if you prefer your meat more well-done.
5. **Rest the steak**: Once cooked to your desired doneness, remove the steak from the grill and let it rest for 5-10 minutes. This helps retain the juices.
6. **Slice and serve**: Slice the carne asada against the grain into thin strips.
7. **Garnish and enjoy**: Sprinkle the sliced carne asada with chopped fresh cilantro and a squeeze of lime juice for added freshness. Serve with tortillas, rice, beans, or your favorite Mexican sides.

Chicken Fajitas

~400 kcal per serving

Servings: 4 | Prep Time: 15 minutes | Cook Time: 15 minutes

Ingredients:

- 1 lb (450 g) boneless, skinless chicken breasts or thighs, thinly sliced
- 2 tbsp (30 ml) olive oil
- 1 bell pepper, sliced
- 1 red onion, sliced
- 2 cloves garlic, minced
- 1 tsp (5 g) ground cumin
- 1 tsp (5 g) chili powder
- 1/2 tsp (2 g) smoked paprika
- 1/2 tsp (2 g) ground coriander
- 1/4 tsp (1 g) ground black pepper
- 1/4 tsp (1 g) ground oregano
- Salt, to taste
- 1 tbsp (15 ml) lime juice
- [Optional] 1/2 tsp (2 g) cayenne pepper (for extra heat)
- 4 small flour or corn tortillas
- Toppings: Fresh cilantro, sour cream, guacamole, salsa, or shredded cheese (optional)

Instructions:

1. **Marinate the chicken** : In a medium bowl, combine the sliced chicken with 1 tablespoon of olive oil, minced garlic, cumin, chili powder, smoked paprika, ground coriander, black pepper, oregano, salt, and lime juice. Mix well, then cover and refrigerate for 15 minutes to allow the flavors to develop.
2. **Cook the chicken** : Heat the remaining 1 tablespoon of olive oil in a large skillet or cast-iron pan over medium-high heat. Add the marinated chicken and cook, stirring occasionally, for 5-7 minutes, or until the chicken is cooked through and lightly browned.
3. **Add the vegetables** : Add the sliced bell pepper and onion to the skillet with the chicken. Stir to combine and cook for an additional 3-4 minutes, or until the vegetables are tender but still crisp.
4. **Assemble the fajitas** : Warm the tortillas on a separate pan or in the microwave for a few seconds until soft.
5. **Serve** : Divide the chicken and vegetable mixture evenly between the tortillas. Top with optional garnishes like cilantro, sour cream, guacamole, salsa, or shredded cheese.
6. **Enjoy** : Fold the tortillas and enjoy your flavorful chicken fajitas, perfect for a family dinner or casual gathering.

Sheet Pan Chicken Enchiladas

Servings: 4 | Prep Time: 15 minutes | Cook Time: 30 minutes

~450 kcal per serving

Ingredients:

- 1 lb (450 g) boneless, skinless chicken breasts or thighs
- 1 tbsp (15 ml) olive oil
- 1 tsp (5 g) ground cumin
- 1 tsp (5 g) chili powder
- 1/2 tsp (2 g) garlic powder
- 1/2 tsp (2 g) onion powder
- Salt and pepper, to taste
- 8 small corn or flour tortillas
- 2 cups (200 g) shredded cheddar cheese
- 2 cups (200 g) shredded mozzarella cheese
- 1 cup (240 ml) red enchilada sauce
- 1/2 cup (120 ml) sour cream
- 1/4 cup (15 g) chopped fresh cilantro
- [Optional] 1/2 cup (75 g) diced red onion or sliced jalapeños for garnish

Instructions:

1. **Prep the chicken** : Preheat your oven to 400°F (200°C). On a baking sheet, drizzle olive oil over the chicken breasts or thighs. Season with cumin, chili powder, garlic powder, onion powder, salt, and pepper. Roast the chicken for 20-25 minutes, or until cooked through and internal temperature reaches 165°F (75°C). Once done, remove the chicken from the oven and let it rest for 5 minutes.
2. **Shred the chicken** : After the chicken has rested, use two forks to shred the chicken into bite-sized pieces.
3. **Assemble the enchiladas** : Lower the oven temperature to 375°F (190°C). Lay the tortillas flat on a clean surface. Evenly distribute the shredded chicken across each tortilla, then roll them up tightly. Place the rolled tortillas seam side down on a baking sheet.
4. **Top with sauce and cheese** : Pour the enchilada sauce evenly over the rolled tortillas, ensuring they are well coated. Sprinkle the shredded cheddar and mozzarella cheese on top of the sauce.
5. **Bake** : Place the baking sheet in the preheated oven and bake for 10-12 minutes, or until the cheese is melted and bubbly.
6. **Garnish and serve** : Remove the sheet pan from the oven. Drizzle with sour cream, and sprinkle fresh cilantro on top. For added flavor and color, you can garnish with diced red onion or jalapeños.
7. **Enjoy** : Serve your delicious Sheet Pan Chicken Enchiladas with a side of Mexican rice or refried beans for a complete meal.

Slow Cooker Carnitas (Pulled Pork)

~350 kcal per serving

Servings: 6 | Prep Time: 10 minutes | Cook Time: 8 hours

Ingredients:

- 3 lb (1.4 kg) pork shoulder (boneless, trimmed of excess fat)
- 1 tbsp (15 ml) olive oil
- 1 medium onion, chopped
- 4 cloves garlic, minced
- 1 tbsp (15 g) ground cumin
- 1 tbsp (15 g) chili powder
- 1 tsp (5 g) oregano
- 1/2 tsp (2 g) ground cinnamon
- 1/2 tsp (2 g) ground cloves
- 1 tsp (5 g) smoked paprika
- 1/2 tsp (2 g) salt
- 1/2 tsp (2 g) black pepper
- 1 cup (240 ml) orange juice
- 1/4 cup (60 ml) lime juice
- 1/4 cup (60 ml) chicken broth
- 2 bay leaves
- [Optional] 1-2 sliced jalapeños for extra heat
- [Optional] Fresh cilantro, for garnish
- [Optional] Warm tortillas, for serving

Instructions:

1. **Prepare the pork** : Trim any excess fat from the pork shoulder and cut it into large chunks to fit into your slow cooker.
2. **Season the meat** : In a small bowl, combine cumin, chili powder, oregano, cinnamon, cloves, paprika, salt, and pepper. Rub the seasoning mixture all over the pork pieces.
3. **Sauté the aromatics** : Heat olive oil in a large skillet over medium-high heat. Add the chopped onion and minced garlic, cooking for about 2-3 minutes until fragrant and softened.
4. **Transfer to slow cooker** : Place the seasoned pork chunks into the slow cooker. Add the sautéed onion and garlic, orange juice, lime juice, chicken broth, and bay leaves. If using, add the jalapeños for an extra kick.
5. **Slow cook the carnitas** : Cover the slow cooker and cook on low for 7-8 hours, or until the pork is fork-tender and shreds easily.
6. **Shred the pork** : Once cooked, remove the pork from the slow cooker and shred it using two forks. Discard the bay leaves and excess fat.
7. **Crisp the carnitas (optional)** : For extra crispy edges, heat a large skillet over medium-high heat. Add the shredded carnitas and cook for 5-7 minutes, occasionally stirring, until crispy and caramelized.

Ground Turkey Tacos

Servings: 4 | Prep Time: 10 minutes | Cook Time: 15 minutes

~290 kcal per serving

Ingredients:

- 1 lb (450 g) ground turkey
- 1 tbsp (15 ml) olive oil
- 1 small onion, chopped
- 2 cloves garlic, minced
- 1 tbsp (15 g) chili powder
- 1 tsp (5 g) cumin
- 1 tsp (5 g) smoked paprika
- 1/2 tsp (2 g) salt
- 1/2 tsp (2 g) black pepper
- 1/2 cup (120 ml) chicken broth
- 1 tbsp (15 ml) lime juice
- 1 tbsp (15 g) tomato paste
- 8 small corn tortillas
- Toppings (optional) :Sliced avocado
- Chopped cilantro
- Diced tomatoes
- Shredded lettuce
- Crumbled queso fresco
- Sour cream
- Salsa

Instructions:

1. **Cook the turkey** : In a large skillet, heat the olive oil over medium heat. Add the ground turkey, breaking it apart with a spoon. Cook for 5-7 minutes until browned and cooked through.
2. **Sauté aromatics** : Add the chopped onion and minced garlic to the skillet with the turkey. Cook for 2-3 minutes until the onion becomes translucent and the garlic is fragrant.
3. **Season the mixture** : Stir in chili powder, cumin, smoked paprika, salt, and pepper. Mix well to coat the turkey evenly with the spices.
4. **Simmer with broth** : Add the chicken broth and tomato paste to the skillet. Stir to combine, scraping up any browned bits from the bottom of the skillet. Let it simmer for 5 minutes, allowing the flavors to meld.
5. **Finish with lime** : Stir in the lime juice, and taste for seasoning. Add more salt or pepper if necessary.
6. **Warm the tortillas** : While the turkey mixture simmers, warm the corn tortillas in a dry skillet or on a hot griddle for 1-2 minutes on each side until soft and pliable.
7. **Assemble the tacos** : Spoon the turkey mixture onto the warm tortillas. Top with your favorite toppings, such as sliced avocado, chopped cilantro, diced tomatoes, shredded lettuce, and crumbled queso fresco.

Beef Enchiladas with Red Sauce

Servings: 4 | Prep Time: 20 minutes | Cook Time: 30 minutes

~380 kcal per serving

Ingredients:

- 1 lb (450 g) ground beef
- 1 tbsp (15 ml) olive oil
- 1 small onion, finely chopped
- 2 cloves garlic, minced
- 1 tsp (5 g) cumin
- 1 tsp (5 g) chili powder
- 1/2 tsp (2 g) paprika
- 1/2 tsp (2 g) salt
- 1/2 tsp (2 g) black pepper
- 1 (10 oz/280 g) can enchilada sauce (red)
- 8 small corn tortillas
- 1 cup (100 g) shredded cheddar cheese
- 1 cup (100 g) shredded Monterey Jack cheese
- 1 tbsp (15 ml) vegetable oil (for frying)
- Toppings (optional): Chopped cilantro
- Sour cream
- Sliced jalapeños
- Diced tomatoes
- Shredded lettuce

Instructions:

1. **Cook the ground beef**: Heat olive oil in a large skillet over medium-high heat. Add ground beef and cook, breaking it apart with a spoon, for 6-7 minutes, or until browned and cooked through.
2. **Sauté the aromatics**: Add the chopped onion and minced garlic to the beef. Cook for another 2-3 minutes until softened.
3. **Season the mixture**: Stir in cumin, chili powder, paprika, salt, and pepper. Mix well to coat the beef evenly with the spices.
4. **Prepare the tortillas**: Heat the vegetable oil in a separate skillet over medium heat. Lightly fry the tortillas one at a time for 10-15 seconds on each side until softened, but not crispy. Drain them on paper towels.
5. **Assemble the enchiladas**: Preheat the oven to 375°F (190°C). Spread a little of the red enchilada sauce at the bottom of a baking dish. Place a tortilla in the dish, spoon a portion of the beef mixture down the center, and top with a small handful of shredded cheese. Roll up the tortilla tightly and place it seam-side down in the dish. Repeat with the remaining tortillas.
6. **Top with sauce and cheese**: Once all enchiladas are assembled, pour the remaining enchilada sauce over the top. Sprinkle the shredded cheddar and Monterey Jack cheeses evenly over the sauce.
7. **Bake the enchiladas**: Bake the enchiladas in the preheated oven for 20-25 minutes, or until the cheese is melted and bubbly..

Pollo Asado (Grilled Marinated Chicken)

~320 kcal per serving

Servings: 4 | Prep Time: 15 minutes | Cook Time: 25 minutes

Ingredients:

- 4 boneless, skinless chicken breasts
- 1/4 cup (60 ml) olive oil
- 1/4 cup (60 ml) fresh lime juice
- 2 cloves garlic, minced
- 1 tbsp (15 g) ground cumin
- 1 tbsp (15 g) chili powder
- 1 tsp (5 g) paprika
- 1/2 tsp (2 g) ground oregano
- 1/2 tsp (2 g) salt
- 1/2 tsp (2 g) black pepper
- 1/4 tsp (1 g) ground cinnamon
- 1/2 tsp (2 g) crushed red pepper flakes (optional, for heat)
- 1 tbsp (15 g) fresh cilantro, chopped (for garnish)
- Lime wedges (for serving)

Instructions:

1. **Prepare the marinade** : In a bowl, combine olive oil, lime juice, garlic, cumin, chili powder, paprika, oregano, salt, pepper, cinnamon, and red pepper flakes (if using). Stir to mix well.
2. **Marinate the chicken** : Place the chicken breasts in a resealable plastic bag or shallow dish. Pour the marinade over the chicken, making sure it's evenly coated. Seal the bag or cover the dish and refrigerate for at least 1 hour, preferably overnight for more flavor.
3. **Preheat the grill** : Heat your grill to medium-high heat (about 400°F/200°C).
4. **Grill the chicken** : Remove the chicken from the marinade and place it on the grill. Cook the chicken for 6-7 minutes per side, or until the internal temperature reaches 165°F (75°C) and the chicken is cooked through.
5. **Serve** : Once cooked, remove the chicken from the grill and let it rest for a few minutes.
6. **Garnish and serve** : Slice the chicken and garnish with fresh cilantro. Serve with lime wedges on the side. Enjoy your flavorful and juicy Pollo Asado!

Shrimp Fajitas

~250 kcal per serving

Servings: 4 | Prep Time: 15 minutes | Cook Time: 10 minutes

Ingredients:

- 1 lb (450 g) large shrimp, peeled and deveined
- 2 tbsp (30 ml) olive oil
- 1 tbsp (15 ml) lime juice
- 1 tbsp (15 g) chili powder
- 1 tsp (5 g) ground cumin
- 1/2 tsp (2 g) smoked paprika
- 1/2 tsp (2 g) garlic powder
- 1/4 tsp (1 g) ground cayenne pepper (optional, for heat)
- Salt and pepper, to taste
- 1 red bell pepper, sliced
- 1 green bell pepper, sliced
- 1 medium onion, sliced
- 8 small flour tortillas
- [Optional] 1/4 cup (60 g) fresh cilantro, chopped
- [Optional] 1/2 cup (120 g) sour cream or guacamole, for serving

Instructions:

1. **Marinate the shrimp** : In a bowl, combine the shrimp, olive oil, lime juice, chili powder, cumin, paprika, garlic powder, cayenne (if using), salt, and pepper. Toss until the shrimp are evenly coated. Let it marinate for 10-15 minutes.
2. **Prepare the vegetables** : While the shrimp is marinating, slice the bell peppers and onion. Set aside.
3. **Cook the shrimp** : Heat a large skillet or frying pan over medium-high heat. Add the shrimp and cook for 2-3 minutes per side, or until they turn pink and are cooked through. Remove the shrimp from the skillet and set aside.
4. **Cook the vegetables** : In the same skillet, add the sliced bell peppers and onions. Cook for 4-5 minutes, stirring occasionally, until they're tender but still slightly crisp.
5. **Assemble the fajitas** : Warm the tortillas in a dry pan or microwave for a few seconds.
6. **Serve** : To assemble, place a few shrimp on each tortilla, top with the cooked bell peppers and onions. Garnish with cilantro, and serve with sour cream or guacamole, if desired.
7. **Enjoy** : Fold the tortillas, and your flavorful Shrimp Fajitas are ready to enjoy!

Baja Fish Burritos

Servings: 4 | Prep Time: 20 minutes | Cook Time: 15 minutes

~450 kcal per serving

Ingredients:

- 1 lb (450 g) white fish fillets (such as cod, tilapia, or mahi-mahi)
- 1 tbsp (15 ml) olive oil
- 1 tsp (5 g) ground cumin
- 1 tsp (5 g) chili powder
- 1/2 tsp (2 g) smoked paprika
- 1/2 tsp (2 g) garlic powder
- 1/4 tsp (1 g) ground cayenne pepper (optional, for heat)
- Salt and pepper, to taste
- 1/2 cup (120 g) all-purpose flour (for coating)
- 2 tbsp (30 ml) vegetable oil (for frying)
- 4 large flour tortillas
- 1 cup (150 g) shredded cabbage (green or purple)
- 1/2 cup (120 g) pico de gallo (fresh tomato salsa)
- 1/4 cup (60 g) sour cream
- 2 tbsp (30 ml) lime juice
- [Optional] 1/4 cup (60 g) cilantro, chopped
- [Optional] 1/4 cup (60 g) hot sauce, for serving

Instructions:

1. **Prepare the fish** : Cut the fish fillets into 1-inch strips. In a small bowl, combine olive oil, cumin, chili powder, paprika, garlic powder, cayenne (if using), salt, and pepper. Toss the fish strips in the spice mixture, ensuring they are evenly coated. Let it marinate for 10-15 minutes.
2. **Coat the fish** : Place the flour in a shallow dish. Dredge each fish strip in the flour, shaking off any excess.
3. **Fry the fish** : Heat vegetable oil in a skillet over medium-high heat. Once hot, add the fish strips in batches and fry for 2-3 minutes per side, or until golden brown and crispy. Remove from the skillet and drain on paper towels.
4. **Warm the tortillas** : While the fish is frying, warm the tortillas in a dry pan or microwave until soft and pliable.
5. **Assemble the burritos** : Spread a thin layer of sour cream on each tortilla, followed by a handful of shredded cabbage. Place 3-4 pieces of fried fish on top. Spoon over some pico de gallo and drizzle with lime juice.
6. **Roll the burritos** : Fold in the sides of the tortillas and roll them up tightly.
7. **Serve** : Garnish with cilantro (if using) and serve with hot sauce on the side for extra kick. Enjoy your Baja Fish Burritos!

Simple Ceviche (Shrimp or White Fish)

Servings: 4 | Prep Time: 20 minutes | Cook Time: 0 minutes (marinating time)

~200 kcal per serving

Ingredients:

- 1 lb (450 g) shrimp or white fish (such as tilapia or cod), diced
- 1 cup (240 ml) fresh lime juice
- 1/2 cup (120 ml) fresh lemon juice
- 1/2 cup (75 g) red onion, finely chopped
- 1 cup (150 g) cucumber, diced
- 1 medium tomato, diced
- 1/4 cup (60 g) fresh cilantro, chopped
- 1-2 fresh jalapeño peppers, finely chopped (optional for heat)
- Salt and pepper, to taste
- [Optional] 1/4 tsp ground cumin or chili powder for extra flavor
- Tortilla chips or tostadas for serving

Instructions:

1. **Prepare the seafood**: If using shrimp, peel, devein, and chop them into small, bite-sized pieces. If using white fish, dice it into small cubes.
2. **Marinate the seafood**: Place the shrimp or fish in a non-reactive bowl. Pour the lime and lemon juice over the seafood until it is fully submerged. Stir gently, then cover the bowl and refrigerate for 2-3 hours, or until the seafood turns opaque and is "cooked" by the citrus juices.
3. **Prepare the vegetables**: While the seafood is marinating, chop the red onion, cucumber, tomato, and cilantro. If you're adding jalapeño for heat, chop it finely and remove the seeds for a milder flavor.
4. **Combine the ingredients**: Once the seafood has marinated, drain any excess liquid from the bowl. Add the chopped vegetables, cilantro, and jalapeño (if using). Season with salt, pepper, and optional spices (cumin or chili powder). Stir gently to combine.
5. **Serve**: Serve your ceviche chilled with tortilla chips or tostadas on the side. Enjoy the refreshing and tangy flavors of this simple ceviche!

Garlic Butter Shrimp Tacos

~350 kcal per serving

Servings: 4 | Prep Time: 10 minutes | Cook Time: 10 minutes

Ingredients:

- 1 lb (450 g) large shrimp, peeled and deveined
- 3 tbsp (45 g) unsalted butter
- 4 cloves garlic, minced
- 1 tsp (5 g) chili powder
- 1/2 tsp (2 g) smoked paprika
- 1/2 tsp (2 g) ground cumin
- 1/4 tsp (1 g) salt
- 1/4 tsp (1 g) black pepper
- 1 tbsp (15 ml) lime juice
- 8 small flour tortillas or corn tortillas
- 1/2 cup (80 g) shredded cabbage (for topping)
- 1/4 cup (40 g) diced red onion (for topping)
- 1/4 cup (40 g) fresh cilantro, chopped (for topping)
- 1/4 cup (60 ml) sour cream or Mexican crema (optional for topping)
- [Optional] Hot sauce or salsa for extra flavor

Instructions:

1. **Prepare the shrimp** : Pat the shrimp dry with paper towels. This helps them sear better when cooking.
2. **Cook the shrimp** : In a large skillet, melt the butter over medium heat. Add the minced garlic and sauté for 1-2 minutes, until fragrant. Add the shrimp to the skillet. Season with chili powder, paprika, cumin, salt, and pepper. Stir well to coat the shrimp in the garlic butter mixture. Cook for 3-4 minutes, flipping the shrimp halfway through, until they are pink and opaque.
3. **Finish with lime** : Remove the skillet from the heat and drizzle the shrimp with lime juice. Stir gently to combine the flavors.
4. **Warm the tortillas** : While the shrimp is cooking, warm the tortillas in a dry skillet over low heat for 30-60 seconds on each side, until soft and pliable.
5. **Assemble the tacos** : Place a few shrimp in the center of each tortilla. Top with shredded cabbage, diced red onion, chopped cilantro, and a dollop of sour cream or crema, if using.
6. **Serve** : Garnish with additional lime wedges, and drizzle with your favorite hot sauce or salsa for an extra kick. Serve immediately and enjoy your delicious, garlicky shrimp tacos!

Veracruz-Style Fish (Pescado a la Veracruzana)

~450 kcal per serving

Servings: 4 | Prep Time: 15 minutes | Cook Time: 20 minutes

Ingredients:

- 4 (6 oz/170 g) white fish fillets (such as snapper, tilapia, or cod)
- 2 tbsp (30 ml) olive oil
- 1 onion, thinly sliced
- 2 cloves garlic, minced
- 1 (14.5 oz/400 g) can diced tomatoes
- 1/2 cup (120 ml) green olives, pitted and sliced
- 1/4 cup (60 ml) capers
- 1/2 cup (120 ml) white wine
- 1/4 cup (60 ml) water
- 1 tsp (5 g) dried oregano
- 1/2 tsp (2 g) ground cumin
- 1/2 tsp (2 g) chili flakes
- 1 tbsp (15 ml) lime juice
- 1/4 cup (40 g) fresh cilantro, chopped (for garnish)
- Salt and pepper to taste

Instructions:

1. **Prepare the fish** : Season the fish fillets with salt, pepper, and cumin on both sides. Set aside.
2. **Sauté the vegetables** : In a large skillet, heat the olive oil over medium heat. Add the sliced onion and cook for 3-4 minutes, until softened. Add the minced garlic and cook for another 1 minute until fragrant.
3. **Add the tomatoes and simmer** : Stir in the diced tomatoes, green olives, capers, and chili flakes. Pour in the white wine and water, then add the oregano. Bring to a simmer and cook for 5-7 minutes, allowing the sauce to thicken slightly.
4. **Cook the fish** : Carefully place the seasoned fish fillets into the skillet, spooning some of the sauce over the fish. Cover and cook for 8-10 minutes, until the fish is opaque and flakes easily with a fork.
5. **Finish with lime** : Drizzle the cooked fish with lime juice and adjust seasoning with salt and pepper if needed.
6. **Serve** : Garnish with fresh cilantro before serving. Serve the Veracruz-style fish with warm rice, tortillas, or your favorite side dish.

Vegetarian Enchiladas with Black Beans

Servings: 4 | Prep Time: 15 minutes | Cook Time: 25 minutes

~320 kcal per serving

Ingredients:

- 8 (6-inch) corn tortillas
- 1 can (15 oz/425 g) black beans, drained and rinsed
- 1 cup (150 g) onion, finely chopped
- 1 cup (150 g) bell pepper, chopped
- 2 cloves garlic, minced
- 1 cup (240 g) enchilada sauce
- 1/2 cup (60 g) shredded cheese (optional)
- 1 tbsp (15 ml) olive oil
- 1/2 tsp (2 g) cumin
- 1/2 tsp (2 g) chili powder
- 1/2 tsp (2 g) paprika
- Salt and pepper to taste
- 1/4 cup (40 g) fresh cilantro, chopped (for garnish)
- [Optional] 1/4 cup (60 g) sour cream

Instructions:

1. **Prepare the filling**: In a medium skillet, heat the olive oil over medium heat. Add the chopped onion and bell pepper, cooking for 5 minutes until softened. Add the minced garlic, cumin, chili powder, paprika, salt, and pepper. Stir to combine, then add the black beans. Cook for another 3-4 minutes until heated through.
2. **Warm the tortillas**: Lightly heat the tortillas on a dry skillet or in the microwave to soften them. This will help prevent them from breaking while rolling.
3. **Assemble the enchiladas**: Preheat the oven to 375°F (190°C). Spread a small amount of enchilada sauce on the bottom of a baking dish. Take each tortilla and spoon a portion of the black bean mixture onto the center. Roll the tortilla tightly and place it seam-side down in the baking dish. Repeat with the remaining tortillas.
4. **Top with sauce and cheese**: Pour the remaining enchilada sauce over the rolled tortillas, ensuring they are evenly covered. Sprinkle shredded cheese on top if desired.
5. **Bake**: Bake the enchiladas in the preheated oven for 15-20 minutes, or until the sauce is bubbly and the cheese is melted.
6. **Serve**: Garnish with fresh cilantro and serve with a dollop of sour cream, if desired. Enjoy your flavorful and satisfying vegetarian enchiladas with black beans!

Sweet Potato Tacos with Chipotle Crema

~350 kcal per serving

Servings: 4 | Prep Time: 15 minutes | Cook Time: 25 minutes

Ingredients:

- 2 medium sweet potatoes, peeled and diced
- 1 tbsp (15 ml) olive oil
- 1 tsp (5 g) ground cumin
- 1/2 tsp (2 g) chili powder
- 1/2 tsp (2 g) smoked paprika
- Salt and pepper to taste
- 8 small corn tortillas
- 1/2 cup (80 g) red onion, finely chopped
- 1/4 cup (40 g) fresh cilantro, chopped
- 1 avocado, sliced (optional) <p>For the Chipotle Crema:</p>1/2 cup (120 g) sour cream
- 1 tbsp (15 ml) lime juice
- 1-2 chipotle peppers in adobo sauce (to taste)
- 1 tbsp (15 ml) adobo sauce from the chipotle can
- 1 tsp (5 g) garlic powder
- Salt to taste

Instructions:

1. **Prepare the sweet potatoes** : Preheat the oven to 400°F (200°C). Place the diced sweet potatoes on a baking sheet, drizzle with olive oil, and season with cumin, chili powder, paprika, salt, and pepper. Toss to coat evenly. Roast in the oven for 20-25 minutes, stirring halfway through, until the sweet potatoes are tender and lightly browned.
2. **Make the chipotle crema** : While the sweet potatoes are roasting, combine the sour cream, lime juice, chipotle peppers, adobo sauce, garlic powder, and salt in a blender or food processor. Blend until smooth and creamy. Adjust seasoning to taste, adding more chipotle for extra heat if desired.
3. **Warm the tortillas** : Heat the tortillas in a dry skillet over medium heat for 30 seconds on each side, or warm them in the microwave covered with a damp paper towel.
4. **Assemble the tacos** : Once the sweet potatoes are done, remove them from the oven. To assemble, place a few spoonfuls of roasted sweet potatoes onto each tortilla. Top with chopped red onion, fresh cilantro, and slices of avocado (if using).
5. **Drizzle with crema** : Finish by drizzling the chipotle crema over the top of the tacos.
6. **Serve** : Serve the tacos warm with extra cilantro and lime wedges on the side. Enjoy these vibrant and flavorful Sweet Potato Tacos with Chipotle Crema!

Veggie Quesadillas

~350 kcal per serving

Servings: 4 | Prep Time: 10 minutes | Cook Time: 10 minutes

Ingredients:

- 4 large flour tortillas
- 1 tbsp (15 ml) olive oil
- 1/2 cup (80 g) bell peppers, thinly sliced
- 1/2 cup (80 g) red onion, thinly sliced
- 1/2 cup (75 g) zucchini, thinly sliced
- 1/2 cup (75 g) mushrooms, sliced
- 1/2 cup (60 g) corn kernels (fresh or frozen)
- 1 cup (120 g) shredded cheese (cheddar, Monterey Jack, or a blend)
- 1/2 tsp (2 g) ground cumin
- Salt and pepper to taste
- Sour cream, guacamole, or salsa (for serving, optional)

Instructions:

1. **Prepare the vegetables** : Heat the olive oil in a large skillet over medium heat. Add the sliced bell peppers, red onion, zucchini, mushrooms, and corn. Season with cumin, salt, and pepper. Cook, stirring occasionally, for about 5-7 minutes, until the vegetables are softened and lightly browned.
2. **Assemble the quesadillas** : Place a tortilla on a clean surface. Evenly spread some of the cooked veggie mixture over half of the tortilla. Sprinkle with 1/4 cup of shredded cheese on top of the vegetables. Fold the tortilla in half to cover the filling, forming a half-moon shape. Repeat with the remaining tortillas and filling.
3. **Cook the quesadillas** : Heat a clean skillet over medium heat. Place one quesadilla in the skillet and cook for 2-3 minutes on each side, or until golden brown and the cheese is melted inside. Remove from the skillet and set aside. Repeat with the remaining quesadillas.
4. **Serve** : Cut the quesadillas into wedges and serve with sour cream, guacamole, or salsa on the side, if desired. Enjoy these veggie-packed, cheesy quesadillas!

Mexican Zucchini Boats

Servings: 4 | Prep Time: 15 minutes | Cook Time: 25 minutes

~280 kcal per serving

Ingredients:

- 4 medium zucchinis
- 1 tbsp (15 ml) olive oil
- 1/2 cup (80 g) onion, chopped
- 1 cup (150 g) corn kernels (fresh or frozen)
- 1/2 cup (75 g) black beans, drained and rinsed
- 1/2 cup (80 g) cherry tomatoes, chopped
- 1/2 tsp (2 g) ground cumin
- 1/2 tsp (2 g) chili powder
- Salt and pepper to taste
- 1/2 cup (60 g) shredded cheese (cheddar, Monterey Jack, or a blend)
- Fresh cilantro for garnish
- Sour cream or salsa for serving (optional)

Instructions:

1. **Preheat the oven** : Preheat your oven to 375°F (190°C).
2. **Prepare the zucchini** : Cut each zucchini in half lengthwise. Using a spoon, scoop out the center of each half to create a boat shape, leaving about 1/4 inch of flesh around the edges. Set the zucchini boats aside.
3. **Cook the filling** : In a skillet, heat the olive oil over medium heat. Add the chopped onion and cook for about 3-4 minutes, until softened. Stir in the corn, black beans, cherry tomatoes, cumin, chili powder, salt, and pepper. Cook for an additional 5-7 minutes, stirring occasionally, until the mixture is heated through and the vegetables are tender.
4. **Stuff the zucchini boats** : Spoon the vegetable mixture into the hollowed-out zucchini halves, pressing down lightly to pack the filling.
5. **Bake the zucchini boats** : Place the stuffed zucchini boats on a baking sheet and sprinkle each with shredded cheese. Bake for 15-20 minutes, or until the zucchini is tender and the cheese is melted and bubbly.
6. **Serve** : Garnish with fresh cilantro and serve with sour cream or salsa, if desired. Enjoy these flavorful, healthy Mexican Zucchini Boats!

Stuffed Bell Peppers with Mexican Rice and Beans

~350 kcal per serving

Servings: 4 | Prep Time: 20 minutes | Cook Time: 35 minutes

Ingredients:

- 4 large bell peppers (any color)
- 1 cup (200 g) Mexican rice
- 1 can (15 oz or 425 g) black beans, drained and rinsed
- 1/2 cup (80 g) onion, finely chopped
- 1 tbsp (15 ml) olive oil
- 1 tsp (5 g) ground cumin
- 1 tsp (5 g) chili powder
- 1/2 tsp (2 g) garlic powder
- 1/2 cup (120 ml) vegetable broth
- 1/2 cup (75 g) corn kernels (fresh or frozen)
- 1/2 cup (50 g) shredded cheese (cheddar, Monterey Jack, or a blend)
- Salt and pepper to taste
- Fresh cilantro for garnish
- Lime wedges for serving (optional)

Instructions:

1. **Prepare the bell peppers**: Preheat the oven to 375°F (190°C). Cut the tops off the bell peppers and remove the seeds and membranes. Set aside.
2. **Cook the rice**: In a medium pot, cook the Mexican rice according to package instructions. Typically, you'll need to sauté the rice in a bit of oil for 2-3 minutes before adding water or broth. Follow the package instructions for the proper cooking time.
3. **Prepare the filling**: While the rice is cooking, heat the olive oil in a large skillet over medium heat. Add the chopped onion and cook for about 3-4 minutes until softened. Stir in the cumin, chili powder, garlic powder, salt, and pepper. Cook for another 1-2 minutes to toast the spices.
4. **Combine the filling**: To the skillet, add the cooked rice, black beans, corn, and vegetable broth. Stir everything together and cook for 3-5 minutes, allowing the flavors to meld and the mixture to heat through. Adjust seasoning with salt and pepper if needed.
5. **Stuff the peppers**: Spoon the rice and bean mixture into each bell pepper, packing it tightly. Place the stuffed peppers upright in a baking dish.
6. **Bake the peppers**: Cover the baking dish with aluminum foil and bake for 25 minutes. After 25 minutes, remove the foil and sprinkle the shredded cheese over the tops of the peppers. Return to the oven and bake for an additional 5-7 minutes, or until the cheese is melted and bubbly.
7. **Serve**: Garnish the stuffed peppers with fresh cilantro and serve with lime wedges on the side for an added burst of flavor.

Mexican Hot Chocolate

~220 kcal per serving

Servings: 2 | Prep Time: 5 minutes | Cook Time: 5 minutes

Ingredients:

- 2 cups (480 ml) whole milk
- 2 tbsp (30 g) unsweetened cocoa powder
- 2 oz (55 g) Mexican chocolate (or use dark chocolate if unavailable)
- 2 tbsp (30 g) sugar (adjust to taste)
- 1/2 tsp (2 g) ground cinnamon
- 1/4 tsp (1 g) ground chili powder (optional, for a spicy kick)
- 1 tsp (5 ml) vanilla extract
- [Optional] Whipped cream or marshmallows for topping

Instructions:

1. **Heat the milk** : In a medium saucepan, heat the whole milk over medium heat until it begins to steam, but do not let it boil. Stir occasionally to prevent it from scorching.
2. **Melt the chocolate** : Break the Mexican chocolate into pieces and add it to the steaming milk. Stir until the chocolate is completely melted and well combined with the milk.
3. **Add cocoa and spices** : Stir in the cocoa powder, sugar, ground cinnamon, and chili powder (if using). Whisk until the mixture is smooth and well combined.
4. **Add vanilla** : Stir in the vanilla extract, and continue heating the mixture for another 1-2 minutes until hot but not boiling.
5. **Serve** : Pour the Mexican hot chocolate into mugs, and top with whipped cream or marshmallows, if desired.

Tres Leches Cake

Servings: 8 | Prep Time: 15 minutes | Cook Time: 30 minutes

~350 kcal per serving

Ingredients:

For the cake:
- 1 cup (125 g) all-purpose flour
- 1 1/2 tsp (6 g) baking powder
- 1/4 tsp (1 g) salt
- 5 large eggs
- 1 cup (200 g) granulated sugar
- 1/2 tsp (2 ml) vanilla extract
- 1/2 cup (120 ml) whole milk

For the tres leches (three milk) mixture:
- 1/2 cup (120 ml) evaporated milk
- 1/2 cup (120 ml) sweetened condensed milk
- 1/2 cup (120 ml) whole milk

For the whipped cream topping:
- 1 cup (240 ml) heavy cream
- 2 tbsp (25 g) powdered sugar
- 1/2 tsp (2 ml) vanilla extract

Instructions:

1. **Preheat the oven** : Preheat your oven to 350°F (175°C). Grease and flour a 9x13-inch baking dish.
2. **Prepare the cake batter** : In a medium bowl, whisk together the flour, baking powder, and salt. Set aside.
3. **Whisk eggs and sugar** : In a separate large bowl, beat the eggs and sugar together until light and fluffy, about 5 minutes. Add the vanilla extract and mix until combined.
4. **Add the dry ingredients** : Gradually fold the flour mixture into the egg mixture, alternating with the milk, until the batter is smooth.
5. **Bake the cake** : Pour the batter into the prepared baking dish and spread it evenly. Bake for 25-30 minutes, or until a toothpick inserted into the center comes out clean. Let the cake cool for 10 minutes.
6. **Prepare the tres leches mixture** : In a bowl, combine the evaporated milk, sweetened condensed milk, and whole milk. Stir until well mixed.
7. **Soak the cake** : Once the cake has cooled, poke holes all over the top with a fork or skewer. Slowly pour the tres leches mixture over the cake, ensuring it soaks into the holes. Let the cake absorb the milk mixture for 30 minutes to an hour.
8. **Whip the cream** : In a large bowl, beat the heavy cream, powdered sugar, and vanilla extract until stiff peaks form.
9. **Top the cake** : Spread the whipped cream over the soaked cake.
10. **Serve and enjoy** : Slice the cake and serve chilled for a delicious and indulgent treat!

Churros with Chocolate Sauce

~400 kcal per serving

Servings: 6 | Prep Time: 20 minutes | Cook Time: 10 minutes

Ingredients:

For the churros:
- 1 cup (240 ml) water
- 2 tbsp (30 g) unsalted butter
- 1 tbsp (15 g) granulated sugar
- 1/4 tsp (1 g) salt
- 1 cup (125 g) all-purpose flour
- 2 large eggs
- 1 tsp (5 ml) vanilla extract
- Vegetable oil for frying
- 1/2 cup (100 g) granulated sugar
- 1 tsp (5 g) ground cinnamon

For the chocolate sauce:
- 1/2 cup (120 ml) heavy cream
- 4 oz (115 g) dark chocolate, chopped
- 1 tbsp (15 g) granulated sugar
- 1/2 tsp (2 ml) vanilla extract

Instructions:

1. **Make the churro dough**: In a medium saucepan, combine the water, butter, sugar, and salt. Bring to a boil over medium heat. Once the butter is melted, remove from heat and stir in the flour until a dough forms. Let it cool for 5 minutes.
2. **Add eggs and vanilla**: Whisk the eggs into the dough, one at a time, until smooth and fully incorporated. Stir in the vanilla extract.
3. **Heat the oil**: In a deep pan, heat about 2 inches (5 cm) of vegetable oil over medium heat to 350°F (175°C).
4. **Shape the churros**: Spoon the dough into a piping bag fitted with a large star tip. Pipe 4-6 inch long strips of dough into the hot oil, cutting them with scissors. Fry in batches for about 2-3 minutes per side, or until golden brown and crispy.
5. **Coat the churros**: Remove the churros from the oil and drain them on paper towels. While still warm, roll the churros in a mixture of sugar and cinnamon.
6. **Prepare the chocolate sauce**: In a small saucepan, heat the heavy cream over medium heat until it begins to simmer. Remove from heat and add the chopped chocolate. Stir until the chocolate melts and the sauce is smooth. Stir in the sugar and vanilla extract.
7. **Serve and enjoy**: Serve the churros warm with the chocolate sauce for dipping. Enjoy your homemade treat with a delightful crunch and a rich, chocolatey dip!

Rice Pudding (Arroz con Leche)

~250 kcal per serving

Servings: 4 | Prep Time: 10 minutes | Cook Time: 30 minutes

Ingredients:

- 1 cup (200 g) long-grain white rice
- 4 cups (960 ml) whole milk
- 1/2 cup (100 g) granulated sugar
- 1/4 tsp (1 g) salt
- 1 cinnamon stick
- 1 tsp (5 ml) vanilla extract
- 1/2 tsp (2 g) ground cinnamon (for garnish)
- [Optional] 1/4 cup (40 g) raisins or dried fruit

Instructions:

1. **Rinse the rice** : Rinse the rice under cold water to remove excess starch. This will help the pudding become creamier.
2. **Cook the rice** : In a medium saucepan, combine the rinsed rice, 1 cup of milk, and a pinch of salt. Bring it to a simmer over medium heat, stirring occasionally. Once it starts to simmer, reduce the heat to low and cook for about 10 minutes, or until the rice is tender and the milk has been absorbed.
3. **Add remaining milk and sugar** : Add the remaining 3 cups of milk and the sugar to the rice mixture. Stir in the cinnamon stick. Bring it to a gentle simmer again, stirring occasionally to prevent the milk from sticking to the bottom. Cook for another 15-20 minutes, until the pudding thickens to a creamy consistency.
4. **Optional step** : If you like raisins or dried fruit, add them in during the last 5 minutes of cooking.
5. **Flavor and finish** : Remove the cinnamon stick and stir in the vanilla extract.
6. **Serve** : Spoon the rice pudding into bowls and sprinkle with a little ground cinnamon on top for garnish.
7. **Enjoy** : Serve warm or chilled. Rice Pudding (Arroz con Leche) is a comforting, creamy dessert perfect for any occasion, offering a lovely balance of sweetness and spice.

Horchata (Sweet Rice Milk Drink)

~150 kcal per serving

Servings: 4 | Prep Time: 15 minutes | Cook Time: 0 minutes

Ingredients:

- 1 cup (200 g) long-grain white rice
- 1/4 cup (40 g) raw almonds
- 1 cinnamon stick
- 4 cups (960 ml) cold water
- 1/2 cup (120 ml) sweetened condensed milk
- 1/4 cup (60 ml) regular milk or almond milk
- 1/2 tsp vanilla extract
- 1/2 cup (100 g) granulated sugar
- [Optional] Ground cinnamon for garnish

Instructions:

1. **Soak the rice and almonds**: Rinse the rice thoroughly under cold water. In a medium bowl, combine the rice, almonds, and cinnamon stick. Add 2 cups of cold water, and let it soak for at least 4 hours or overnight for the best flavor.
2. **Blend the mixture**: After soaking, drain the rice and almonds, then transfer them to a blender. Add the remaining 2 cups of cold water. Blend on high for 1-2 minutes until smooth and creamy.
3. **Strain the horchata**: Using a fine mesh sieve or cheesecloth, strain the mixture into a large pitcher to remove the rice and almond pulp. Press the mixture with a spoon to extract as much liquid as possible.
4. **Add sweetness**: Stir in the sweetened condensed milk, regular milk (or almond milk), vanilla extract, and sugar. Mix well until the sugar is completely dissolved.
5. **Serve**: Pour the horchata over ice in tall glasses.
6. **Garnish and enjoy**: Optionally, sprinkle with a dash of ground cinnamon for extra flavor. Sip and enjoy this refreshing, creamy Mexican treat!

Flan (Mexican Caramel Custard)

Servings: 6 | Prep Time: 15 minutes | Cook Time: 1 hour

~230 kcal per serving

Ingredients:

- 1 cup (200 g) granulated sugar
- 1/4 cup (60 ml) water
- 1 can (12 oz/355 ml) evaporated milk
- 1 can (14 oz/396 g) sweetened condensed milk
- 1/2 cup (120 ml) whole milk
- 4 large eggs
- 1 tbsp vanilla extract
- Pinch of salt

Instructions:

1. **Prepare the caramel** : In a medium saucepan, combine the sugar and water. Cook over medium heat, stirring occasionally, until the sugar has melted and turned a golden amber color. Be careful not to burn it.
2. **Caramelize the pan** : Once the caramel is ready, quickly pour it into a round flan dish (or a 9-inch round cake pan), swirling the pan to coat the bottom evenly. Let it cool and harden while you prepare the custard.
3. **Make the custard** : In a large bowl, whisk together the eggs, evaporated milk, sweetened condensed milk, whole milk, vanilla extract, and a pinch of salt. Mix until smooth and well combined.
4. **Pour the custard into the pan** : Slowly pour the custard mixture into the flan dish over the set caramel.
5. **Bake the flan** : Preheat your oven to 350°F (175°C). Place the flan dish into a larger baking dish and fill the outer dish with hot water, creating a water bath. Bake for 50-60 minutes, or until a knife inserted into the center comes out clean.
6. **Cool the flan** : Let the flan cool to room temperature, then refrigerate for at least 4 hours or overnight to firm up.
7. **Serve** : To serve, run a knife around the edges of the flan to loosen it, then carefully invert it onto a plate. The caramel will flow over the custard, creating a beautiful sauce.

Pineapple Tamales (Tamales de Piña)

~220 kcal per serving

Servings: 12 | Prep Time: 45 minutes | Cook Time: 1 hour 30 minutes

Ingredients:

- 2 cups (240 g) masa harina (corn flour for tamales)
- 1/2 cup (115 g) unsalted butter, softened
- 1/2 cup (100 g) sugar
- 1/2 tsp vanilla extract
- 1/2 tsp baking powder
- 1/4 tsp salt
- 1 cup (240 ml) pineapple juice
- 1 cup (150 g) pineapple, finely chopped
- 1/4 cup (60 g) sweetened condensed milk
- 1/2 cup (120 ml) whole milk
- 1 package (about 20) corn husks, soaked in warm water for 30 minutes

Instructions:

1. **Prepare the masa dough** : In a large mixing bowl, combine the masa harina, butter, sugar, vanilla extract, baking powder, and salt. Mix well.
2. **Add liquids** : Gradually pour in the pineapple juice, sweetened condensed milk, and whole milk. Stir until the masa dough becomes smooth and soft. The consistency should be slightly wet but firm enough to hold its shape.
3. **Add pineapple** : Fold in the finely chopped pineapple, ensuring it is evenly distributed throughout the dough.
4. **Prepare the tamales** : Take a soaked corn husk and spread a spoonful of the masa mixture on the center, flattening it slightly. Fold the sides of the husk over the masa, then fold up the bottom of the husk, creating a little pocket to secure the tamale.
5. **Steam the tamales** : Place the tamales upright in a large steamer, with the open ends facing up. Cover them with a wet cloth or more corn husks to retain steam. Steam over medium heat for 1 to 1.5 hours, or until the masa is fully cooked and pulls away easily from the husk. Add water to the steamer as needed during the cooking process.
6. **Serve** : Let the tamales cool slightly before serving. They are perfect as a sweet dessert or a treat for special occasions.

Fried Ice Cream with Cinnamon Sugar

Servings: 4 | Prep Time: 30 minutes | Cook Time: 5 minutes

~320 kcal per serving

Ingredients:

- 4 scoops vanilla ice cream
- 1/2 cup (60 g) cornflakes, crushed
- 1/4 cup (30 g) shredded coconut
- 1/4 cup (50 g) chopped pecans or almonds
- 1/2 cup (120 ml) heavy cream
- 1/4 cup (30 g) all-purpose flour
- 1 large egg
- 1/2 tsp vanilla extract
- 1/4 tsp ground cinnamon
- 1/2 cup (100 g) sugar
- Oil for frying (vegetable or canola oil)

Instructions:

1. **Prepare the ice cream**: Scoop the vanilla ice cream into 4 equal balls. Place them on a baking sheet lined with parchment paper and freeze for at least 2 hours, or until firm.
2. **Make the coating**: In a shallow dish, combine the crushed cornflakes, shredded coconut, and chopped nuts. In a separate bowl, whisk together the flour, egg, heavy cream, and vanilla extract to form a smooth batter.
3. **Coat the ice cream**: Roll each frozen ice cream ball in the batter, ensuring it is completely covered. Then, roll it in the cornflake mixture, pressing gently to coat it evenly. Repeat the process for each scoop.
4. **Freeze again**: Return the coated ice cream balls to the freezer for another 30 minutes to an hour to ensure the coating sets.
5. **Fry the ice cream**: Heat oil in a deep fryer or large pot to 375°F (190°C). Carefully lower one ice cream ball at a time into the hot oil. Fry for 20-30 seconds, or until golden brown and crispy. Remove with a slotted spoon and drain on paper towels.
6. **Prepare the cinnamon sugar**: In a small bowl, mix together the sugar and ground cinnamon.
7. **Serve**: Sprinkle the cinnamon sugar over the fried ice cream and serve immediately while still warm and crispy. Enjoy!

Margarita Mocktail (Non-Alcoholic Option)

~120 kcal per serving

Servings: 2 | Prep Time: 10 minutes | Cook Time: 0 minutes

Ingredients:

- 1/2 cup (120 ml) fresh lime juice
- 1/4 cup (60 ml) orange juice
- 1/4 cup (60 ml) agave syrup or simple syrup
- 1/4 cup (60 ml) sparkling water or club soda
- Ice cubes
- Salt for rimming glasses
- Lime wedges for garnish
- [Optional] 1-2 tsp lemon zest for extra citrus flavor

Instructions:

1. **Prepare the glasses** : Start by rimming two glasses with salt. To do this, rub a lime wedge along the edge of each glass, then dip it into a plate of salt.
2. **Mix the mocktail** : In a cocktail shaker or mixing glass, combine the fresh lime juice, orange juice, and agave syrup (or simple syrup). If you want an extra zesty kick, add the lemon zest.
3. **Shake** : Fill the shaker with ice and shake well for about 10-15 seconds to combine the ingredients.
4. **Serve** : Fill the prepared glasses with ice and pour the mixture evenly into both glasses.
5. **Top with sparkling water** : Pour sparkling water or club soda into each glass to add some fizz.
6. **Garnish and enjoy** : Garnish each drink with a lime wedge and serve immediately. Enjoy your refreshing, non-alcoholic Margarita Mocktail!

Printed in Dunstable, United Kingdom